BITCOIN

Getting Started Guide On This New Era
Of Digital Currency

The Best Crypto Investing Book You
Must Need

Includes Pro Tips All You Need To
Know

OSCAR R. GUTIERREZ

CONTENTS

INTRODUCTION

Bitcoin: A Brief Histories

Bitcoin is the only cryptocurrency that's been around for more than seven years. It has also experienced widespread adoption, but it took a while to reach this point. Before Bitcoin existed, several cryptocurrencies gained some degree of acceptance. The story began in 1980 when the cryptographer David Chaum first developed the idea of a cryptocurrency backed by a proof of work computer algorithm rather than central banks. Chaum later created DigiCash, a brief, unsuccessful attempt to become the first widely-used cryptocurrency. US E-gold is one of the most famous Bitcoin-precursor cryptocurrencies. However, technologically, it was a far cry from Bitcoin because it had a central owner and a non-fixed supply.

The month of August was 2008 when Neal Kin, Vladimir Oksman, and Charles Bry filed a patent application to patent an encryption technology. Domain name Bitcoin.org was registered the same month using anonymousspeech.com, allowing anonymous domain name registration.

The most important day was the 31st of October, 2008, when Satoshi Nakamoto (a pseudonym with a real identity that is not yet confirmed) released a white paper called "Bitcoin: A Peer to Peer Electronic Cash Systems." The report discussed various applications for the coin, providing details about blockchain technology and how it can be mined using computer algorithms. The paper's original purpose was to use Bitcoin as an example of a deflationary currency in that governments and other central lenders cannot intentionally increase the amount of money available; thereby, the currency would be devalued. The paper also discussed the problems with banks as trustworthy lenders and how the irreversible nature of transactions on Bitcoin can reduce the risks of fraud for merchants.

In January 2009, people began mining coins before the first Bitcoin blocks were made. Nakamoto and other cryptography enthusiasts began trading the currency for services. In October 2009, an official exchange rate was set for the coin at USD$1 equals 1,309.03 BTC. The exchange rate was initially determined by the amount of power it would take to mine one Bitcoin.

The first transaction in the real world was in May 2010, when the enthusiast Laszlo Hanyecz purchased two pizzas in Jacksonville, Florida, for 10,000 BTC. The value of 10,000BTC today is more than $40 million. A few months later, in August, the first significant Bitcoin hacking incident occurred; the hacker took advantage of a flaw within the Bitcoin verification system and created an estimated 184 billion bitcoins. This caused the first-ever significant drop in the worth of Bitcoin as an asset. It also led to government inquiries into the possibility of money laundering that Bitcoin could facilitate. The initial fears did not last long, however. November 2010 saw Bitcoin reach a market cap of one million dollars for the first time.

In January 2011, Bitcoin received proper coverage from mainstream media. Silk Road, an underground dark web site dealing with illegal goods, such as illicit prescription drugs and stolen credit cards, was created based on receiving and sending payments using Bitcoin. It was estimated that as high as 50 per cent of Bitcoin transactions were made via Silk Road. The illusion of anonymity that surrounds Bitcoin

It became a popular choice among Silk Road users. February saw Bitcoin reach a value of $1 for the first time, and by July, the price had risen to $31.

2012 was an uninteresting year, but the real-world acceptance continued by hosting platforms WordPress accepting Bitcoin in November. In march 2013, the market value was $1 billion. Bitcoin exchange Coinbase has reported more than 1 million transactions in just one month. In June, the DEA announced 11.02 Bitcoins as assets in a drug seizure. This was the first time a government agency acknowledged Bitcoin as having intrinsic value. Drugs continued to draw attention in the months following. When Silk Road owner Ross William Albrecht was detained in October. During the arrest, the FBI took the equivalent of 26,000 Bitcoins taken from Silk Road servers. More positive news followed the following month when the initial Bitcoin ATM opened in Vancouver, and China was introduced in the year. Chinese market activity outpaced that of the US at first. In November 2013, the cost of one Bitcoin was $1000 for the first time.

December 2013 saw China's central bank's decision that Bitcoin was not a form of currency and prohibited financial institutions from accepting Bitcoins as a payment method. February saw Japanese Mt. Gox stop Bitcoin withdrawals due to technical problems. In just a few months, Gox declared bankruptcy based on claims of poor management and the absence of proper security protocol.

Around $740 million worth of Bitcoin, approximately 77% of the total amount of Bitcoin in circulation, was destroyed during the incident. The issue resulted in Bitcoin's value Bitcoin decreasing by 36% during the time.

The month of June was when TeraExchange LLC received approval from the U.S.Commodity Futures Trading Commission. This was the first time a U.S. agency had approved a Bitcoin exchange. Computer maker Dell started accepting Bitcoin as a form of payment in 2000, the most significant business to accept it up to this date. AirBaltic also became the only airline that carried Bitcoin payments. In December, the tech giant Microsoft started accepting payments in Bitcoin.

Coinbase, one of the most popular cryptocurrency exchange platforms, received 75 million dollars in a financing round that included The New York Stock Exchange as a small investor. The real-world scaling continues; by August 2015, more than 160,000 companies accepted Bitcoin as a payment method. December was the month that brought news of the possible identity of the famous SatoshiNakamoto character. Wired magazine reported that the Australian Craig Wright was indeed Nakamoto. The publication triggered events that eventually confirmed that Wright wasn't Nakamoto .July 2016 was the second "halving day" in the history of Bitcoin when the payout for mining one block was reduced from 12.5 bitcoins for each block. The reason for this was Bitcoin's initial concept to reduce the number of new coins on the market gradually. This halving process is scheduled to happen in 2020, with the entire supply accessible to the market by 2140.

As of the date when this article was written, Bitcoin trades for around $4,000 on exchanges.

The basics of Blockchain Technology

While it is possible to write the entire time reading about Blockchain and the technology that underlies it, It is essential to know the basics when considering investing in Bitcoin or another cryptocurrency.

Blockchain is a decentralized ledger. That is, it's a document available to all and can easily be checked by any. This is essential for all non-tangible goods since, unlike tangible goods such as candy or socks and candy, we require an account of the transaction occurring if there is a problem. For instance, we need evidence that Steve paid John to buy the socks John bought from him. The blockchain will be able to provide an account of the transfer from Steve's account to John's and not anyone else's.

Before that, we'd recourse to a third party like a bank to confirm that the transaction did take place. The bank would then calculate the percentage of the transaction. Since the bank's information is not available to the public, we have to believe that the bank has done its task. With blockchain technology, we've got an infallible and 100% reliable document of the transaction that took place; anyone could observe this. Also, the middleman does not need to pay a substantial extra fee. The only cost involved is the expense of managing the blockchain.

If we are using blockchain to facilitate financial transactions, it is highly beneficial to countries with an established banking system. Every transaction is stored as a block with a date and a timestamp. The blocks are not able to be changed without the entire community seeing. The issue this resolves is commonly referred to as the "double- spending issue," in which cryptocurrency and other digital currencies (like cryptocurrency) can be used more than once. Blockchain technology allows us to see that Steve has already spent funds to make payments to John, and he cannot then apply that money to try to pay Sally. The blockchain builds trust among the parties involved. Trust is essential when it comes to transactions involving money.

Blockchain's applications aren't only financial. Blockchain can also be used to store any other information we require in a freely accessible, transparent, readable format. This could be anything from voter records during an election or a self-executing agreement between two parties that is fulfilled the contract when both parties have fulfilled their obligations. Blockchain removes the requirement for a middleman or an independent auditor in these instances since the technology is both an auditor and an independent. In theory, blockchain technology could substitute lawyers, accountants, and a large portion of the financial services sector. Before we get too excited, many of the blockchain's non-financial applications remain in the abstract.

What is the process behind Bitcoin Function?

Bitcoin is the digital currency that adheres to the same threerules traditional or fiat currencies adhere to.

- They should be challenging to make (cash) or tolocate (gold as well as other rare metals)

- They must have a restricted amount of food

- Other people must acknowledge them as beingvaluable

    If we look at Bitcoin, it ticks every one of the three traits:

- Bitcoin employs sophisticated algorithmic computer programs, requiring much computational power and proof-of-work. Therefore, it can't be duplicated quickly or at a lower cost

- To be precise, there is an unending amount of Bitcoins 21 million. At the time of writing, around 1/3 of the total were mined.

- There are a myriad of Bitcoin trading platforms, and Bitcoin is accepted as payment everywhere, from Subway to OKCupid

Bitcoin miners are motivated to mine because they get Bitcoin as an incentive for their work. Bitcoin was developed to be a deflationary currency, which means that the quantity of money is set as opposed to fiat currency. This, along with the decentralization concept, guarantees that no individual or the government can make more coins once the supply is exhausted. The currency's value will theoretically increase when all coins have been produced.

Bitcoin transactions are stored on a digital ledger (or record) called the blockchain. The fundamental principle that supports the validity of Bitcoin is decentralization. Because of decentralization, the Bitcoin blockchain is not the property of only one individual or company. Everyone has access to the blockchain. So transactions are broadcast over the internet to ensure that both parties can participate.

They have abided by their side of the accord. It is an open- source code (like Linux or Android Operating Systems) which means that anyone can look it up, guaranteeing transparency for all parties.

Decentralization lets the blockchain be protected by multiple entry points and backed up with several sources of failure. This prevents situations like theft or hacking. For instance, if someone offers you a Bitcoin, you could look up the blockchain's records to verify that the Bitcoin is legal and hasn't been used before. This method means we don't require third parties to confirm the transactions. The only transaction costs arise from the energy or mining power needed to run the blockchain.

It has wide-ranging real-world applications, from making it easier to make international transactions (since Bitcoin has no nationality) to decreasing the price of certain products.

Bitcoin as a Store of Wealth

The fact that Bitcoin is an inflation-proof currency is beneficial when fiat currencies are experiencing massive amounts of inflation. Similar to gold, which has traditionally

been utilized during times of economic distress, Bitcoin has the potential to perform the same. Bitcoin can meet specific requirements to be used as an asset to store value or money.

- It must not be perishable.

- It should not be depreciated over time.

The second point is controversial since critics claim that Bitcoin may decline due to technology that is better than it. But, Bitcoin has now reached the end at which it is of value, similar to email or Facebook. It's not particularly beneficial in the case of being the only one with an address you can send mail to; however, the more people who use Bitcoin, the simpler and more valuable it becomes.

Venezuela is currently experiencing the biggest cash-flow crisis of the past decade. The inflation rate has reached a point where people's currency is nearly worthless compared to the US dollar. A large proportion of the population is unable to pay for essentials. Except for those who have Bitcoins valued against the US dollar keeps increasing.

For different reasons, China has been doing precisely the same as the US. Traditional investments with Chinese assets have earned lower than in previous years because of the devaluation of the Yuan. The conversion of money into gold and silver is a strict process and usually comes with significant transaction charges. Bitcoin isn't affected by any of these problems and is often the best alternative for those seeking to protect their wealth in the short and longer term.

Gold has been the most common backup plan, as well as a "hedge" against the uncertainty of markets for financial instruments. Prices are likely to increase when there is war or a financial crisis.

When financial markets fall, it is a sign of weakness. But, in recent years, this is not the instance. Since this article was written, gold's 12-month performance has stagnated while Bitcoin has increased by almost 1000 per cent. The rising tensions inside North Korea are just one reason for Bitcoin's rise during periods of uncertainty.

The regional tensions have led to increased purchases by China, Japan, and South Korea. Chinese, Japanese, and South Korean markets.

Bitcoin Myths Common toBitcoin Debunked

Like any technological innovation, there are various things that people who aren't well-informed don't understand. This is why misinformation gets out that creates confusion, fear, and uncertainty and can harm the advancement of technology.

❖ **Bitcoin is not legal**

Let's tackle the major issue right off the bat, won't we? A central bank not back a currency isn't a reason to make it illegal. You, the user using it as virtual money, Bitcoin is legal as it is used to purchase legal products.

❖ **Developers or miners may alter the number of Bitcoins accessible to them to gain**

The Bitcoin algorithm operates ensures that there are no shortcuts to finding one. If a fake Bitcoin cannot meet all the criteria, all transactions made with it will be refused. Similar to the way banks refuse counterfeit banknotes.

❖ **Bitcoin isn't worth much because any centralgovernment does not back it**

Like every currency, they're only worth what a person will be willing to pay to them. In the same way, gold and US dollars do not have any intrinsic significance, and Bitcoin isjust a way to exchange.

❖ Bitcoin's primary purpose is to aid criminals, and the government will take it off the market

At one point, an enormous portion of Bitcoin use was for illicit activities. Much of this was carried out through Silk Road's black market underground site. But, that is not the case anymore. Bitcoin is now accepted by more than One hundred sixty thousand merchants worldwide, and acceptance continues to increase. Technology's benefits like reduced transaction fees have more significant applications for large financial institutions than for a basement resident who is twenty years old and trying to purchase LSD from a man in a different country. It's important to remember that fiat currencies can also be employed for criminal activities.

It also relies on the notion that Bitcoin is entirely private. There aren't designated Bitcoin accounts; however, each Bitcoin account is unique, and each transaction is documented on an open ledger (the blockchain). Thus, with some research, you can identify the person behind a Bitcoin transaction.

If a possible government shutdown is concerned, it's somewhat more complex. The government can make life tough for those solely dealing in Bitcoin However, and this issue is limited to taxes on Bitcoin.

❖ 21 million Bitcoins isn't enough of a number to be used to make it practical for everyday use

What is lacking is that it cannot calculate the fact that Bitcoin is divisible by the eight decimal places. 0.00000001 BTC is the lowest unit that is available. It is also called 1 Satoshi. There are 2,099,999,997,690,000 (just over two quadrillions) maximum possible units or Satoshi in the Bitcoin system. If 1 Bitcoin is too large for daily transactions, we'll shift to smaller units to make it easier, Similar to how we currently use pennies to make small transactions.

❖ Hackers could take all Bitcoins

It's crucial to distinguish between hacking websites and exchanges and the blockchain itself being hacked. Hackers can exploit the security vulnerabilities of private firms, whereas blockchains are not centralized, so there isn't a security flaw that hackers could take advantage of. Similar reasoning can also be used to defend the US dollar. However, the fact that an establishment is robbed doesn't mean that there is a chance that the US dollar was stolen from its source. But, you must be aware of the security measures you should take when you store your Bitcoin, likemaking a secure, offline wallet.

❖ Bitcoin is a Ponzi/Spin-off scheme

My most-loved. Pyramid schemes are the game of zero-sum. Early adopters and the creators benefit from the money poured into the program by the late adopters. With Bitcoin, everybody can help regardless of what time it was when they made their first investment. Another misconception could be that Bitcoin is the primary founder of Bitcoin. Bitcoin is decentralized. There isn't any "CEO" or another person in the highest position.

❖ **Bitcoin is dead, and there is no reason to invest in Bitcoin today.**

I've seen at least "Bitcoin deaths" over the last five years. From hacking-related incidents up to Silk Road Founder Ross William Albricht's detention, critics have used these incidents to fuel Bitcoin's declining value. The numbers aren't lying, though. They show that Bitcoin is much better than ever regarding the market value and actual world acceptance.

In 2012, commentators declared it was " too late" for investors to bet on Bitcoin. But, the actual adoption is growing, and the cost continues to rise. Does that mean there won't be problems shortly? I'm confident they will.

If, however, Bitcoin transactions continue to increase and the currency is not showing indication of slowing anytime soon.

Latest Bitcoin Innovations: SegWit,Lightning Network

The biggest technical challenge Bitcoin is confronted with in its history is the problem of scaling. In other words, its capacity to handle the increasing volume of transactions. Currently, each Block of transactions on the Bitcoin network is 1MB, equivalent to 10 minutes of transaction time, which increases during times with heavy users. This benefits large financial institutions because 10 minutes is far faster processing than SWIFT and other payments networks. However, 10 minutes is a lengthy and inefficient payment time for smaller companies, such as cafes.

Over the years, the continuous debate has been about the most effective method of increasing Bitcoin's block size. The longer these debates continue, the more time passes before any feasible solutions are developed. There are two camps: those who support an abrasive fork that loosens the rules of the protocol and those who prefer an easy separation that is more restrictive of regulations of the protocol currently in use.

Without getting into technical details, people who favour an open fork suggest a solution called Segregated Witness, or SegWit. The premise behind SegWit is that a transaction's signature (or witness) could be stored in separate blocks about the transaction itself, which frees up block space for further transactions. The witness's information is secured and can't be changed, meaning it is impossible to alter the sender's information. This can be of great use in decreasing the risk of hacking the transaction.

Like any change that could be made, there's a degree of uncertainty. In terms of practicality, SegWit activation will affect the value of Bitcoin in one way or another in the near term. However, when this article was written, SegWit had only been activated for less than hours, and its price was stable.

In the event of its activation, SegWit could pave the way for the lightning network, a technology that allows immediate Bitcoin transactions. Fast transactions

As previously mentioned, Bitcoin will aid, greatly facilitate micro and nano transactions as previously stated, and allow small-scale businesses to reap the benefits of accepting the payment method of Bitcoin at the point points of sale. This is particularly beneficial for countries with weak fiat currencies. An example currently in use is Venezuela, in which it is the case that the Venezuelan Bolivar was able to lose about 90 per cent of its value against the USD US dollar in less than one year.

Bitcoin transactions help the small but significant percentage of the Venezuelan public hold the value of their currency.

What exactly is Bitcoin Cash?

Bitcoin Cash (BCH or BCC on exchanges) is a spin-off cryptocurrency created due to the August 1st hard fork made by only a tiny but significant portion of my members. The separation results in increased block sizes and quicker processing times, resulting in fewer transaction fees. The block size has grown to 8MB from the 1MB initially that Bitcoin makes use of. This fork was created to address the issues of scalability that Bitcoin is currently facing.

If Bitcoin Cash is more technologically advanced than Bitcoin, why shouldn't I invest in it instead? It's difficult to answer, as we are still in the beginning stages. As of this writing, the fork is barely one month old, and Bitcoin Cash has had high price fluctuation. The liquidity is smaller than Bitcoin (meaning it's hard to market large quantities), and the actual results are still to be determined. If you're beginning to invest, Bitcoin Cash is certainly something you should be watching. But the effects of the network Bitcoin remain too powerful to ignore, and it's still pretty popular as the top cryptocurrency.

As for market prices and market value, price is a factor. Bitcoin Cash split on August 1st initially caused a drop in the value of Bitcoin; however, it reached an all-time high in the latter part of August. The value of Bitcoin Cash initially dropped before a surge, then reset to the current price of around $550.

If you bought Bitcoin before August 1, Bitcoin Cash should be treated as a distinct currency. The transaction in Bitcoin won't be duplicated to Bitcoin Cash or vice versa. If you want to purchase Bitcoin, search for BTC when you exchange. If you bought Bitcoin before August 1, you could be eligible to get the same quantity as Bitcoin Cash - providing you kept it in a wallet that wasn't linked to an exchange.

For miners or anyone interested in mining at the time of this writing, Bitcoin Cash provides higher rewards for mining compared to Bitcoin due to a lower difficulty in its proof-of-work algorithm.

How do I purchase Bitcoin

There is no longer a time when purchasing Bitcoin was a long and a bit uncomfortable experience. Buying Bitcoin is similar to transferring currencies when you go to a vacation spot.

There are two methods to purchase Bitcoin. The first option is using fiat currency (USD, EUR, GBP, etc.).) to buy Bitcoin using an exchange. Exchanges work in the same way that traditional foreign currency exchanges do. Prices fluctuate daily, as do conventional markets for the business of currencies; they are available 24 hours a day. They earn money by charging a small amount for every transaction.

Some charge buyers and sellers, while others charge an amount for purchasing. To protect themselves, most of these exchanges require you to verify your identity before allowing you to buy cryptocurrency.

It is essential to know the types of payments the exchange will accept. Some accept credit or debit card transactions, while others only accept PayPal or wire transfers from banks. Below are three of the most popular and reliable currency exchanges to buy Bitcoin, Ethereum, and other altcoins using fiat currencies like US dollars or Euros. British Pounds.

Coinbase

The largest exchange of currency worldwide, Coinbase allows users to purchase, sell and store cryptocurrency. Coinbase is, without doubt, the most accessible exchange for those looking to participate in this market. They allow trading on Bitcoin, Ethereum, and LiteCoin using fiat currencies. The conversation is known for its outstanding security measures and policies concerning the storage of money. They also have a fully functional iPhone and Android application for trading and buying at the touch of a button, which is extremely helpful if you're seeking to trade.

Once you've verified, signed in, and completed the identity verification procedure, you can immediately purchase Bitcoin by debit or credit card.

How to Safely Keep YourBitcoin

Congratulations on buying your very first Bitcoins! Once you've purchased your Bitcoin, it is essential to ensure it's safe. This can be done by taking it off the exchange into the Bitcoin wallet. The term "wallet" signifies that you can do precisely the same thing as you could with a traditional wallet. You can check how much Bitcoin you've got and then use it to spend the Bitcoin you have. A key distinction is that, since Bitcoin is decentralized and is stored on the Blockchain, the wallets cannot "store" the Bitcoin as such.

In 2011, Tokyo, the Tokyo-based Bitcoin trading platform Mt. Gox experienced losses of up to $27.2 million, and 80,000 users suffered losses of more than $460 million in Bitcoin when the exchange was hacker-infested. Mt. Gox wasn't a fly-by-night night operation, either. In fact, at the time, it was the most powerful trading platform for cryptocurrency on Earth. However, inadequate security procedures and poor management allowed the attacks to happen. The company ultimately declared bankruptcy in the wake of allegations of fraud. A large portion of the stolen coins is not found to date. This is why it's crucial that if you wish to store your cash over the long term, you keep them safe.

To understand the concept of wallets, we must first know how they function. Bitcoin transactions require encryption keys (from the sending party) and private keys (from the receiving) for processing correctly in the Blockchain.

Public keys are a set comprised of between 26-35 alphabetic characters e.g. [1Co5CmEZNz35Am59EcFhKGRdNfLrzppGkJ](#)

If you can give this address to someone else who has it, they can send money to your account. It's safe to disclose your private key, also known as your wallet's address, to anyone since they will only be able to deposit funds in your account using this data. A 2013 student at a university was awarded

22 Bitcoins (then in the amount of about $20,000) by holding the sign with his public key in the form of QR codes during the ESPN edition of College Gameday.

Your private key, however, must be kept by you only. Don't give your private keys to anyone else.

There are a variety of wallets available. This is a list of each.

❖ **Desktop Wallets**

Desktop wallets are an ideal way to move your Bitcoins away from exchanges without carrying any additional details like the paper or physical wallet. Think of them as the equivalent of a Bitcoin bank account you can access on your personal computer. Most desktop wallets protect your private keys to give you extra protection. This article will briefly overview some of the most well-known desktop Bitcoin wallets. The wallets listed below are free; you don't need to pay for a desktop wallet.

❖ **Electrum - https://electrum.org**

Although its design might not be a winner, Electrum does the job it's designed to. This code can be downloaded as open source, meaning it's less likely that the team was developing it will slip into something malicious. Electrum lets you keep and spend your Bitcoins in a relatively straightforward manner. It offers the benefit of having your private keys stored offline and allowing you to go online while in "watching exclusively" mode, meaning that if your computer is compromised during this process, attackers will not be able to use any bitcoins. It also supports different hardware wallets.

❖ **Exodus - https://www.exodus.io/**

In contrast to Electrum, Exodus is not an open source. However, Exodus does have the benefit of storing other

coins, such as Ethereum, Litecoin, and Dogecoin, as well as Bitcoin. The interface is also much more friendly to use than Electrum.

It is important to note that because desktop wallets require computers to connect to the Internet, they may not be completely secure.

❖ **CoPay https://copay.io**

CoPay is available on mobile and desktop platforms, making it a great choice when you want to make purchases or receive Bitcoins while on the move. CoPay needs multiple signatures (ways to verify your account) to make transactions and is a security feature. It also has a multi- user option, which can benefit families and groups.

The fact that the software's code is free of charge is an advantage.

❖ Paper Wallets

Paper wallets are documents of the private keys you write down on paper. They often have QR codes so they can be quickly scanned by the person sending them and send bitcoin.

Pros:

* Cheap

Private keys aren't stored in a digital format, so they are safe from cyber-attacks and hardware malfunctions.

Cons:

* Paper is lost because of human error

* Paper is delicate and could rapidly degrade in specific environments.

It is not easy to pay for cryptocurrency in a short time if needed not suitable for daily transactions

Using paper, you can use sites such as bitaddress.org to make non-secure digital wallets. They are classified as not secure since you need to connect to the Internet to utilize them. If the website is compromised, hackers could gain access to the private keys of every single one ever made.

Step by Step Instructions on how to make a 100 100% secure paper wallet

The material you need is required.

- Offline download of bit address -http://bit.ly/offlinebitaddress

- Lili Live USB - http://www.linuxliveusb.com/en/download

- Ubuntu Operating System -
  http://www.ubuntu.com/download/desktop

- USB Flash Drive - either brand new or that you'reprepared to
  format your existing information from

- A printer

Installation of Ubuntu onto your flash driveDownload the programs
mentioned above

2.   Open LiLi, then insert your USB flash drive into your
computer.

3.   In Lili, select a source, and choose the "ISO/IMG/Zip"option.

4. Then, in Lili Options - select "Format the key to FAT32."

5.   Download the offline Bitaddress and place it in your flashdrive.

Remove your personal computer's connection to the internet. This is
to ensure that you are unable to allowsomeone else can gain access to
your computer when you are creating an encrypted key.

Ubuntu booting Ubuntu using your flash drive

Reboot your PC and press F12 just before Windows or OSX starts.
Choose USB HDD in the start menu. Then, run Ubuntu from the
flash drive. Ubuntu operating system on the flash drive. After it has
loaded, select "Try Ubuntu."

After Ubuntu is installed after it has loaded, go to the System settings, then printers, and select your printer. Print one page to verify that it is connected.

Create your wallet

6.   Select the Firefox icon on Ubuntu, and you will open the private browsing window.

7.   Type the following in the address bar: file:///cdrom/bitaddress.org-master/

8. Click on "BitAddress.org.html."

9.   Move your cursor until the timer is at zero (this will verify that you're a natural person)

10. Choose Paper Wallet

Follow the steps below to create your wallet from paper.

Transfer BTC by using the public address that is located on the left part of the wallet (represented by the QR code)

Additional Recommendations

It is recommended to keep your wallet's paper in a bag sealed with plastic to shield it from water or humid conditions—print multiple copies for added security. And if you're holding cryptocurrency over the long term, put the paper in a secure.

Hardware Wallets

Hardware wallets are physical storage devices that include your private keys. The most commonly used form of them is secure USB sticks. These are similar to the kind you make on your own. However, someone else has established these security procedures for you. This is especially beneficial for those who do not have the technical expertise. Many include backup software built to protect you if you lose your keys.

They use two-factor authentication or 2FA to ensure that only the wallet owner can access the information. For instance, one of the factors could be a physical USB stick that you plug into your computer. The second is a 4-digit PIN - similar to using a debit card to take money out of an ATM.

Pros:

* Nearly impossible to hack at the date of this writing, there are ZERO instances of hardware wallets

If a virus or malware infects your computer, your wallet will not be accessible because of 2FA

This remote code will never leave your device nor transfer to a computer. So yet again, malware or computers infected are not a problem.

* Can be carried around with your bag if you want to use your money with cryptocurrency

It is easier to make transactions using cash wallets made of paper

* Store multiple addresses on one device. This is ideal if you intend on using several Bitcoin accounts

*   For the gadget-lovers of your life, they're a lot more stylish than a piece of paper

Cons:

*   Costs more than wallets made of paper - beginning at about $60

*   Easily damaged by hardware degrading and changes to Technology

* Different wallets work with different cryptocurrency

*   Trusting that the service will provide a wallet that is not in use. Utilizing a second-hand wallet is a huge security risk. Make sure you purchase your hardware wallets only from authorized sources.

The most well-known among them are wallets like the Trezor as well as the Ledger wallets. Both offer users an intuitive experience and an easy and safe way to keep your Bitcoin.

How to trade Bitcoin

If you decide to keep Bitcoin in the long run, You may also want to trade it in exchange for other cryptocurrencies or fiat currencies. This is the quickest method to earn money with Bitcoin; however, it is also the riskiest. If you want to trade Bitcoin for fiat currency, it is possible to sell It at the current exchange rate at the exchange you purchased them from, such as Coinbase and Kraken.

If you are looking to trade them in exchange for other currencies, it is best to transfer the coins onto Poloniex or another business such as

Bittrex. You'll find the exchange rate for Bitcoin and various currencies when you are on there. It is important to note that this might differ from the exchange rate that applies to the Bitcoin to fiat pairing. For instance, the exchange rate for BTC in exchange for Litecoin (LTC) could differ from that for LTC/USD or BTC/USD. Fees are generally very low for transactions between crypto and crypto; however, the maximum rate on Poloniex, for instance, is 0.25 per cent.

Another aspect being considered is the liquidity of specific pairs. For instance, you do not want your transaction delayed because the exchange isn't selling the quantity of the coin you are purchasing. To check the liquidity of specific coin pairings, go to http://coinmarketcap.com

They also allow you with prices of the past for the different pairings and also their liquidity (ease of trading) for every market.

As with all speculative markets, you are investing in Bitcoin is risky. You could lose money. This is particularly true when trading on emotion rather than rationale. It is recommended to act cautiously and conduct your research before doing any kind of trading in real. You can practice with virtual money (known as paper trading) on sites like https://www.whaleclub.co/

You'll indeed be prone to mistakes when you first start. Learn from your errors. However, it's vital to do it with funds you can afford to make a loss.

If you plan to trade, you should take interim profits to yourself. So, the gains you've achieved are in your account, not on paper. Averaging the cost of a dollar also applies to trading, in addition to investing.

What determines the price of Bitcoin?

If you decide to bet on Bitcoin or any other cryptocurrency in general, it's crucial to comprehend the factors in the market that affect prices one way or the other. Numerous frequently interact with each other; however, for the sake ofsimplicity, we'll go over each one at a time.

China

A country with more influence on the value of Bitcoin is China. More fiat-to-Bitcoin trades originate from China as compared to any other, and many of the biggest exchanges around the globe are located in China. Around 70% of global Bitcoin transactions occur in China. Chinese market.

Positive news from China is positive news for the market all around. An announcement in December 2013 from China's People's Bank of China decreeing that Bitcoin is not an acceptable currency sank the market by 35% in less than an hour. However, the reports of Bitcoin being accepted by Chinese businesses often increase the Bitcoin price.

One of the main reasons China is an essential player in this Bitcoin industry is the Chinese government's strict financial regulations on assets that the Chinese Yuan holds. Middle and wealthy Chinese citizens are seeking an option to ensure their financial security without relying on the values of the Yuan that have been diminished in recent years. Bitcoin is the ideal solution to accomplish this. Furthermore, Yuan devaluation could increase Bitcoin development shortly.

Russia

Like China, Russia is also experiencing problems with its ruble currency. The ruble has declined to the US dollar for the last three years.

Years. In this way, Russians want to safeguard their wealth by converting their rubles to Bitcoin.

Acceptance of Bitcoin in Russia has also been a critical participant in Bitcoin fluctuations in price. In May 2017, the announcement that Ulmart, the most prominent internet retailer in Russia, would start accepting Bitcoin payments drove the market to a record high of $1800.

Government Regulation

Support from the government for Bitcoin can play in the cost of the cryptocurrency as a commodity. While Bitcoin isn't connected to any specific country, for its widespread adoption to happen, it will require the government's support. The biggest issue facing governments is currently Bitcoin's apparent "complete security" and its connection to criminality, particularly tax avoidance. Once the measures are implemented to remove the element of anonymity (regardless of the moral stance regarding this), government support will grow, and so will the value of Bitcoin.

In contrast, whenever there is news of a clampdown on Bitcoin, whether as a virtual currency or on a technological level - the price goes down

Technological Innovation

Innovations within technological advancements within the Bitcoin network are essential to ensure that it continues growing in value. As we've mentioned before, new developments such as SegWit and the light network help with scaling issues and improve the growth of Bitcoin in a technological sense.

The capacity of the cryptocurrency to manage micropayments (transactions with a small value) is a crucial aspect that has a significant impact on future value. The block size of 1MB restricts the system's efficiency in handling micropayments, which results in the minimum amount of transactions and delays in processing payments when you make excessively many transactions at once.

The team hopes to implement the lightning network to alleviate these problems and increase Bitcoin's actual world viability.

Mass Media

Contrary to what we'd like, most of the population still receives their information from only one or two sources. For the record, the mainstream media doesn't comprehend Bitcoin, not one bit. Because of the absence of suitable cryptocurrency or cryptocurrency journalists in significant publications, they'd prefer to air good news stories such as "Bitcoin may reach $100,000 in five years" or, in reverse, "Bitcoin is the largest market since the dot-com boom" instead of examining it at the level of technology, or concentrate on the innovations that have been developed. Positive coverage of Bitcoin in the media can lead to new investors, while negative news causes an increase in the value.

The flip side is that specific Bitcoin experts have already formed their minds without considering the technology.

Financing for Blockchain Companies

As blockchain-related companies continue to attract more funds and investments, the currency gets more legitimacy.

Many blockchain-related startups accept the acquisition of Bitcoin and other cryptocurrencies, including Ethereum.

Middle-Class Investors

A factor that is often ignored. Although Bitcoin might be growing in popularity with younger investors and even larger institutions, it's far from being considered by the American upper middle classes. For example, consider Tom, 55 years old and from Maryland. He's married and earns an income of just six figures from his higher management position. His portfolio is currently comprised mainly of blue-chip stocks and low-interest index funds. He's not aiming to hit many homers, and he's trying to build up his retirement funds. When Bitcoin is established as a kind of "digital gold" and becomes a reliable long-term investment, rather than a speculative play as some big institutions see it, its worth will only increase. That's why we'll need more people like Tom as our primary Bitcoin buyers for the value to continue to grow.

Technical Analysis

It is essential to note the traditional analysis of technical aspects or chart analysis as one would perform on stocks is complex because it is) just eight years old, so it's not complete information. It is) unlike anything else we've experienced before.

But charting has an important place within the Bitcoin world. I recommend that you learn the books on technical analysis for stocks in case you plan to trade Bitcoin at a high level, and candlestick charts are the most effective to sell on the cryptocurrency market.

Mass Adoption

The more businesses are willing to accept Bitcoin as a form of payment, the more Bitcoin is recognized as the currency. The scalability issue with Bitcoin will be the primary factor in this. The adoption rate is not slowing down, and the number of businesses accepting the currency is growing. If giant corporations like Amazon and Apple started accepting Bitcoin payments, the price would increase again.

Bitcoin to Business: What Your Company can benefit from accepting Bitcoin Payments

If you're not currently a small company owner, you can leave this section out, but should you be one, I would advise you to be attentive.

In the first place, accepting Bitcoin transactions can help you save money. In contrast, traditional credit card processing is around 2 per cent. Utilizing

Bitcoin payment services like BitPay can lower these fees to a minimum of one per cent. A tiny percentage reduction such as this can result in huge savings over the long term. Suppose you're an online retailer frustrated by banks charging exorbitant fees for conversions of currency or just desire to make your item or service more accessible to all customers. In that case, Bitcoin might be the solution for you. Bitcoin does not discriminate against countries; transactions from all countries are subject to the same transaction fees.

Millions of Bitcoin users are searching for ways to spend their cash, and adding your company to the mix can benefit the entire network. Bitcoin users are enthusiastic, and they love supporting businesses that accept Bitcoin. The cryptocurrency market is growing in popularity, and making your company an early adopter allows you to become an industry leader by gaining brand recognition.

You also have protection from fraudulent chargebacks. Since Bitcoin payment transactions cannot be reversed, you, the merchant, are not responsible for the cost of fraud.

For non-profit organizations, Bitcoin donations have soared each year since its beginning.

The Jamaican Bobsled team funded their journey for the Olympic Winter Olympics entirely from cryptocurrency donations. It also benefits customers by knowing the total amount of their offering and how it's allocated in a market where transparency is paramount.

If you're concerned about the volatility of Bitcoin's price, then services such as BitPay can help you with regular bank transfers to the local currency.

Can I Still Earn Money using Bitcoin In 2017?

The short answer is yes.

The long answer is that Bitcoin continues to grow both as a virtual asset and as an alternative currency that can be used in real-world applications. The growing globalization and the need to transfer funds across borders will increase Bitcoin's popularity. The volume of cross-border money transfers continues to grow yearly and accounts for almost one per cent of the global GDP. The total market value of Bitcoin is $71 billion, higher than that of other countries such as Costa Rica and Bulgaria.

Bitcoin's close (but not totally) anonymity is another reason that continues to propel its growth. This is crucial in countries such as China, where governments strictly regulate fiat currencies.

Bitcoin is now an entire brand itself. It is a symbol of the digital store of worth. This is something that no other cryptocurrency could do. Imagine it as purchasing a house. Do you prefer to buy one in a "name name" city such as London or New York, where the demand for homes like yours will always be high regardless of the economy? For the same amount in Oklahoma City, where you may have the chance to purchase an even bigger home, however, will you be in a position to sell it in the event of a downturn in the market?

Suppose you're looking to use Bitcoin as an instrument to trade and exchange with other cryptocurrencies or as longer-term storage of value. In that case, Investing on sites like Coinbase or Kraken has also been much more accessible.

But remember that nobody thinks they are an expert and ahead of trend whenever the price is up. There will be down times, and it's crucial to take care of your risk to endure the down times and make a profit in the best ones. Keep in mind that even the most successful people in the industry can get it wrong from time to time

A Bitcoin-Investing Mentality as well as Strategies to Reduce Your Risk In a market that is as volatile as crypto, it's essential to limit your risk to the greatest extent possible. With average market volatility of 10% daily, this is essential to protect your investment portfolio and security.

The first rule is to never put money into something you cannot manage to shed. It's tempting to think you can hit an inning-winning home run, but you'll end up with exhausted nights and anxious days.

Also, unless you're trading daily, you shouldn't be checking crypto price charts every couple hours. It will only cause an additional source of anxiety. The price could fluctuate in large percentages every day. It's the nature of the Bitcoin market. But, be aware that the price has been increasing over the long term.

Dollar Cost Averaging

One of the most effective ways to reduce the risk of an unstable market is to utilize the "dollar cost average. This means dividing the total investment you plan to make and purchasing Bitcoin regularly instead of doing it all at once.

In the case of dollar cost averaging, you're simply purchasing less of an investment (in this instance, Bitcoin) when the price is high and more when it is low. The real risk is reduced because you're only subject to a portion of any market decrease, in contrast to all the risk of an investmentin lump sums. The cost per coin is likely to be less.

Let's take an example. Alan John and John had $1200 invested in investing in Bitcoin at the beginning of the year. Alan decides to support the entire $1200 by January 1st. John, however, chooses to utilize the dollar cost average. He will make a $100 investment at the beginning of each monthand will invest an overall total of $1200. The prices in this scenario are actual Bitcoin trading rates as of these dates.

January 1st, 2015 1st, 2015 $305.32 February 1st 2015

$237.18 March 1st, 2015 - $263.57 April 1st , 2015 -- $255.23 May 1st, 2015 May 1st 2015 $226.45

June 1st, 2015 1st June 2015 $233.44 July 1st, 2015 $260.73 August 1st, 2015 - $260.73 1st August 2015 -$283.04

September 1st, 2015 September 1st 2015 $229.00 October 1st, 2015 - - $240.10 1st November 2015 $125.28 - $325.28

December 1st , 2015 $375.95 - $375.95

Alan's investment total in BTC is 3.93 (1200/305.32). John's overall investment in BTC is 4.55 (1200/269.60)

The price on January 1st, 2016 -- $433.57

Alan's Portfolio Value = 3.93*433.57 = $1704.02 John's Portfolio Value = 4.55*433.57 = $1974.37

Alan's ROI = 42%.

John's ROI is 64.5 percent

Thus, using the dollar cost averaging method, John's mean BTC purchase cost was $269.60, much more than Alan's, paid an all-in lump sum of $305.32. Because of a lower average purchase cost, John's ROI is higher over time. Alanpurchased her coins at the top of the market before an extended decline, while John used the recession to benefit.

Keep in mind that the time spent in the market is better thanthe market by a long margin. In general, the more time you're invested in something more.

FOMO and FUD

You must be familiar with two terms if you intend to invest and trade in Bitcoin or any other cryptocurrency.

FOMO - Fear of Not Being able to Access

This is evident in news stories about The number of Bitcoin

transactions increasing by 100+% per day. It's tempting to trade a portion of (terrible notion) your Bitcoin to get the latest trending cryptocurrency, but it's hazardous. Most smaller altcoins are backed by purely theoretical technology and do not have any actual use in the real world for the product or service it is supporting. Make sure you do your research on cryptocurrency news. Even if the headline says, "Amazing Altcoin tied with Amazon deal," it isn't necessarily a guarantee that the deal is even closer and that there's even an agreement. Be sure to verify the facts before you invest.

It is crucial to realize that Bitcoin is now at an age where it has practical applications and is the most popular cryptocurrency. Thus, Bitcoin has more market saturation and is less likely to appreciate as much as smaller coins. It's the same with Bitcoin. But with huge rewards comes significant risk. Smaller coins can and often do lose as much as 80percent of their value within a matter of days (for additional information, refer to our Chaincoin pumps and dump plan of July 2017); however, Bitcoin remains strong. If you're planning to purchase and keep just one coin over the long run, Bitcoin should be your only choice.

FUD is Fear, Uncertainty, and Doubt

FUD is the propagation of misinformation through uninformed sources. A lot are the sources that have perverse motives behind this. They may want to spread the idea of alternative currency or might have traded (bet on the declining price) Bitcoin. Of course, Bitcoin's legitimate criticism as innovation is acceptable and is good if the technology improves. FUD, however, is mostly slander and false assertions regarding Bitcoin as existing technology, the people behind it, or those who invested in it.

What can you do to avoid confusion? Simple, by getting the latest information about Bitcoin and other news about cryptocurrency from trustworthy sources who don't have any vested interests either way. It is essential to utilize several sources to gain an accurate and complete market picture.

How to invest your Bitcoin - Icos

An ICO (also known as Initial Coin Offering is an alternative crowdfunding method that numerous blockchain startups have adopted in the last few months. Instead of giving dollars for company shares, the patrons can donate Bitcoin or another cryptocurrency in exchange for tokens for the business.

The most well-known ICO to date was the Ethereum ICO of July 2014. Ethereum is a blockchain-based platform that allows applications and automated contracts, also known in the industry as "smart contracts," to be built upon. Ethereum received roughly 31,500 Bitcoin during the funding stage, equivalent to $18.4 million. In exchange, 60 million Ethereum tokens were given to those who participated in the fund. The project was very effective in the short run; today, 60 million Ethereum is worth about $24 billion.

The ICOs are a method for businesses to finance their blockchain-related projects and generate investors with a return. Usually, the offerings last for several weeks, and the company releasing the new tokens will set a target amount they intend to raise. They have seen an exponential increase in popularity over the past 18 months. 2017 is expected to be the year in which blockchain-based companies have raised more funds from ICOs than conventional venture capitalists. As an investment tool, they allow savvy investors to take the first steps in a new and exciting venture.

The downside is that so many new ICOs appear; some are less credible than others. If you're investing in an ICO, follow the venture's primary purpose and not any fancy marketing jargon that the company employs in its marketing copy. The fact that something is built on a blockchain-based platform doesn't necessarily mean a real need to purchase the service or item. Another thing to look at is the developer team behind the project and their experience in successfully developing blockchain-based applications.

As with any typical startup project, more ICOs fail than achieve success, and raising funds is not the only element of a successful venture. One example of an ICO that has been issued is Bancor, and the ICO was conceived to make an automated market-making (generating a computerized buy and sell price) product that could provide an exchange for the digital asset. The project raised $153 million in just three hours, more than 50% more than its initial goal.

However, the project ran into issues when it came to accepting investors' transactions along with being able to take the Bancor team issuing additional tokens when the financing period was over. This means a lower return for investors. Like all investments, conducting the necessary research before getting involved is crucial. Never invest more than you could afford to risk losing. Lastly, as with any other asset within the Bitcoin or cryptocurrency market, ICOs aren't an opportunity to make money fast.

Recently, the ICO excitement has become so intense that ICOs are using Facebook advertisements and celebrity endorsements to try and gain investors. You should ask yourself whether you'd invest in a non-blockchain business through a Facebook advertisement. I'm guessing you have the answer. If a company's most crucial feature includes "amazing returns" instead of technological advancement, it's most likely to be an unwise investment instead of one that's worth your money.

The other aspect you must be aware of is that you are not purchasing stock of these businesses during their ICO phase. You do not own any part of the company's shares, and you hold the tokens they use, which are likely to fluctuate in value due to external factors affecting the company's performance.

Why I Can't Recommend You Use Bitcoin

If Bitcoin's price increases (and this happens often!), the question of mining is always asked. It is usually from those without experience or looking for a "free" method to grab an ounce from the cake.

The whole thing begins with a variation on this question.

"Why should you Bitcoin at $100, $1,000, or $4,000 when you can use computers to mine Bitcoin for no cost?"

As with all other things - there's nothing free about Bitcoin.

As we've previously mentioned, the method by which Bitcoins are made and "mined" is using computers to tackle an ever-more complex set of algorithms. The users are then rewarded for completing these algorithms by receiving Bitcoin. No human power is involved, and you aren't required to solve the algorithm. You need to connect your computer with the Bitcoin network, which will do the rest. There are no shortcuts or breakthroughs, and the only method Bitcoin can be obtained faster is by using more power on your computer. How much computing power you provide determines the amount of your payout. The more force you give, the tremendous amount of Bitcoins you will receive.

Here's the main reason mining is an investment unsuitable for the familiar Joe.

. Costs for electricity - The power costs associated with operating your computer continuously (which is essential to mine) significantly outweigh any Bitcoins you earn in exchange for the work. It is necessary to have access to industrial electricity rates of approximately $0.02 per kWh for your business to succeed at a low scale.

. Needing specialist hardware - Today, one of the fastest mining processes needs special hardware called application-specific integrated circuits (ASIC). ASICs are classified as supercomputers that can only accomplish one thing. ASICs that are specialist Bitcoin ASIC miners available for consumers to purchase begin at about $1000 and can go up to $2000-$2000.

$2500.

Maintenance of equipment - Maintaining all of this computing power is an additional expense. The cooling cost is a significant expense that must be accounted for in long- term profit. The hardware that is running continuously burns out quicker as well. Replacement mining machines are likely to be required at some point.

The growing dimension of the Bitcoin network is that the network will pay out an amount fixed in Bitcoin regardless of the number of miners on the web. At present, the rate of payment is 1800 BTC per day. This may sound like a large number until you consider how many miners are in the Bitcoin network. The current mining power amounts to approximately 17.6 billion desktops. So the average amount paid to the user running a desktop computer for a full day is about $0.000107 every day. That's about 2 cents per calendar year's worth of BTC. There is a higher chance of winning the lottery than earning a profit mining Bitcoin, the standard computer at home.

The mining industry in 2017 will be a different process than in 2010 or 2012. A few opportunities included investment into Bitcoin farms or purchasing group processing capacity of ASIC at a discounted price. This is also known as a "mining pool" or "mining pool." Due to lower power costs, most global mining pools are located in China, and Iceland has the second highest amount. Mining pools require an investment that is lower initially, but they need low electricity rates and have a questionable ROI.

It's also important to note that many of the people who promote cloud mining or group mining are doing so as part of an affiliate program associated with the company they're marketing, which means that they receive an % of the commission each when someone joins.

For the ordinary Joe with a small amount of money, I strongly suggest purchasing coins rather than mining them. It is more likely that you will earn more in the short and longterm.

Is there a Bitcoin ETF or Mutual Fund I could invest in?

Exchange Traded Funds (ETFs) and mutual funds have been among the most secure investments in recent years. Instead of investing in single firms, you're purchasing the entire shares of multiple businesses. If you allow this type of diversification, you can make the lowest risk of using your money. Investors have been demanding a Bitcoin or cryptocurrency fund similar to this because of the price fluctuation of various cryptocurrencies.

However, attempts to create the creation of a Bitcoin ETF have been thwarted by regulatory agencies so far. In 2017 the two Bitcoin ETF applications were rejected by the SEC. The reason given by the agency was the absence of regulations and surveillance of the market in the cryptocurrency space.

The closest to an actual Bitcoin mutual fund is a broad- based fund provided by http://thetoken.io in Russia. The fund comprises 16 distinct cryptocurrency tokens, including Ethereum (22 per cent) and Bitcoin (17 per cent), the two most significant components that make up the funds. The fund can be invested using both BTC and ETH, and the funds are kept in Ethereum-protected wallets. However, investments in fiat currency aren't currently supported. An intelligent contract secures the fund on the Ethereum platform to guarantee the authenticity of the offered tokens.

However, the biggest drawback of this site is that it's not accessible to people within the US or Singapore, but this could change shortly depending on the regulation status for Bitcoin and other cryptocurrencies. Like all investments, you can lose money during a market recession, so onlyinvest funds you're comfortable losing.

Ten Commandments of Bitcoin Ten Commandments of Bitcoin

If you don't get anything else out of this publication, make sure to adhere to these principles to be placed in a much better place to earn more money than the other investors just starting.

. Then, be a believer in Bitcoin in a technological sense

. It is forbidden to give your private keys to anyone otherthan yourself

. Keep yourself updated on Bitcoin information fromreliable sources

. You should not panic-sell in the downturn

. It is best always to make the intermediary profits to benefitoneself

. It is your responsibility to store cryptocurrency in a securemanner

. Do not waste your time every hour scouring thecryptocurrency market

. It is forbidden to make Bitcoin on their desktop computer

. Do not invest more than you could afford to lose

o. Always be there to help those who have less educationthan you.

What is Cryptocurrency?

Based on who you ask, the concept of cryptocurrency could prompt responses from "the future's money" to the level of "the largest bubble since DOTCOM inflation." US Senator Thomas Carper summed it up best in layman's phrases.

"Virtual currencies, the most famously Bitcoin, have caught the attention of a few, provoked terror in others, and frightened the hell out of all of us."

To give a more precise understanding, the term "cryptocurrencies" is currencies that don't have a central bank, such as a central bank for a country. They are created by methods of encryption that restrict the number of monetary units (or coins) that are made and then verify the transfer of money after they have been made.

This creation method is known as "mining" because of its theoretical similarities to the process of mining gold or various other valuable metals. To extract cryptocurrency, you must solve a more complicated system or puzzle. The method of solving these algorithms requires lots of computer processing power. It costs money to mine them, and we aren't able to create value out of air. Thus, these currencies and their worth are protected by the laws of mathematics and not any central bank or central government.

As cryptocurrency's popularity grows, so does the amount of actual-world applications. Everything from physical products like vouchers, gift cards for sporting events, and even hotel reservations can be bought using cryptocurrency.

Restaurants and bars are now accepting cryptocurrency as a form of payment. Many NGOs accept donations made in Bitcoin and other cryptocurrencies in addition.

Additionally, there are illegal uses, such as underground marketplaces selling illegal products like Silk Road and AlphaBay.

They have a wide variety of advantages over currencies that

We use and know that we are familiar with and use. That's why they're popular with investors who are long-term as well as short-term investors and speculators. As with all investments, cryptocurrencies have their drawbacks. We will look at them in the next section of this book.

A Brief Background ofCryptocurrency

Although the actual applications of cryptocurrency go back just seven years, the technological aspects date from another 30 years back to the 1980s.

The cryptographer David Chaum was the first to propose a cryptocurrency after he developed an algorithm for encryption that could allow secure, non-destructible exchanges between two people.

Chaum later established DigiCash, one of the first companies to produce currency units based on his algorithm. It is important to remember that only DigiCash, the DigiCash company, could create the coin, different from Bitcoin and other cryptocurrencies, where anyone can make money (providing they possess the computing capability). After encountering legal issues and rescinding a deal with Microsoft that would have had DigiCash integrated into each home Windows operating system, DigiCash was declared bankrupt in the mid-90s.

Chinese computer engineer Wei Dai published a white paper on "b-money" that set the groundwork for the structure behind cryptocurrency we have today. The form provided information on complex algorithms, privacy for buyers, and decentralization. The currency, however, did not come to fruition.

US-located E-Gold was a second unsuccessful attempt to create a cryptocurrency in the early 1990s. The Florida E- Gold company offered its customers e-gold "tokens" to exchange for their old trinkets, jewellery, and coins. These tokens were then exchanged in exchange for US dollars. The site was initially popular and had over one million active accounts as of the mid-2000s. One of the first strategies employed by E-Gold is that anybody could sign up for an account. This led to numerous frauds that were facilitated on the site. Additionally, inadequate security procedures led to some hacking attacks, and the company ended up closing in 2009.

The modern cryptocurrencies used today started with Bitcoin, initially described by an anonymous entity (the identity of which has not been verified as a single individual or group), Satoshi Nakamoto. Bitcoin was made available to the public in early 2009, and a large community of people began to mine, invest in, and trade the cryptocurrency. First, the Bitcoin market was created in February of 2010.

In 2012, the Hosting and web development platform WordPress was the very first big retailer to allow payments in Bitcoin. This was crucial since it gave Bitcoin authentic credibility in the marketplace and proved that big corporations believed in Bitcoin as an alternative currency.

The Cryptocurrency and Traditional Currency. Traditional Currency

Understanding Currency: worth of any coin is decided by the amount people will give to you for the currency.

Any cryptocurrency, currency, or other requires three simple guidelines:

They must be hard to make (cash) or to locate (gold as well as other metals of a precious nature)

They must have a restricted quantity

Humans around the world should acknowledge them as being valuable

Utilizing just Bitcoin (BTC) for an illustration, the currency can tick the boxes for the following three characteristics:

Bitcoin is a complex system of algorithmic computer program in its creation that requires lots of computing power, which means it can't be easily replicated or even at a bargain

There's only a limited amount of Bitcoins - 21 million to be precise[22. In 2015, approximately 1/3 of the total were mined.

There are a myriad of Bitcoin Exchanges addition, Bitcoin is accepted all over the world, starting from Subway to OKCupid

What makes cryptocurrency different from traditional currencies (also called Fiat the money) is that they are not tied to a specific nation, state, or institution (in the majority of instances). There aren't USA Bitcoins, no Japanese Litecoins, or something similar. They are not centralized.

Bitcoin was created as a "deflationary currency," meaning its value could naturally increase as time passes. Contrary to fiat currencies, which are prone to inflation and whose value is likely to decrease. In 1917, for instance, one dollar was about $20.17 in 2017. Therefore, you can say that today, the US Dollar was worth 20 times less than one hundred years ago. If you hold onto one dollar over 100 years, you'll be able to buy smaller and smaller items to exchange it for, while when you use Bitcoin, that will not occur.

For a second real-world instance. On the 22nd of May, 2010, Laszlo Hanyecz completed the first cryptocurrency transaction in real-time by purchasing two pizzas in Jacksonville, Florida, for 10,000 BTC. Today, 10,000BTC isworth $40 million.

Bitcoin was created to ensure that no single person (or the government) could make a greater quantity of money while reducing the value of money already on the market.

It is also essential to remember that the fiat currencies we recognize and cherish weren't always the most critical participants in the world of money. For centuries, gold and other precious metals were considered the most desired daily currency. It wasn't until the government could standardize and verify the metallic content of the coins (andlater, paper bills) that they became the most popular choice for people.

The legendary economist John Maynard Keynes said this about inflation and currency inflation.

"By an ongoing cycle characterized by inflation, governmentofficials can take the bulk of their people's income in secret and without notice. Through this process, they do not just confiscate and take away arbitrary amounts of money; although the process afflicts some, it also benefits certain. The thought of this arbitrarily change in wealth does not strike just insecurity, but faith in the fairness of the currentdistribution of wealth."

Although Bitcoin is a subject of uncertainty surrounding it, founded on the principle of decentralization, The real value lies in looking at it from a different angle. As no single entity is accountable for the distribution of money, the system obligates all participants (government, businesses, and consumers) to make clear their operations, reducing the possibility of fraud and manipulation. Transparency is assured by paying miners for their work (in the form of coins). This is the primary reason why investors are confident in the longevity that the cash will have.

A common argument used by Bitcoin opponents is that since there is no official backing for this currency, the system can completely fail in the future. We have witnessed this happen sometimes using fiat currencies in the context of hyperinflation in which governments no longer guarantee their money's worth and, as a result, need to develop a new currency. The most common examples are the German Weimar Republic in the 1920s, in which the coin could not hold its value, and notes were used to wallpaper. Today, it is reported that the Venezuelan economy is expected to experience more than 1000% inflation this year, making many of the country's citizens unable to pay for basic needs such as bread. Bitcoin people see Bitcoin as a hedge against recession.

The expense associated with international trade is another aspect where cryptocurrency has a significant advantage over conventional ones. Anyone required to transfer money abroad knows that the payment for processing these transactions could exceed the limits.

Sometimes, these charges can reach 10%. In other words, as Bitcoin does not look at the international transaction (as there aren't "nations" in the trade) differently than local ones. There are no fees to send money to any region of the globe. Transaction speed between countries is also significantly faster than conventional fiat currencies. The average Bitcoin transaction can take about 10 minutes to process instead of days to process international transfers, and other coins can process transactions much quicker.

UNDERSTANDINGBLOCKCHAIN TECHNOLOGY

How is this money worth anything even? It's all in blockchain technology. If you are planning to invest any money whatsoever in cryptocurrency, you must have an understanding of blockchain technology and theapplications it has.

Blockchain technology can provide an incorruptible, permanent document of all transactions that have occurred and is free of human error or loss of data. It is essential to keep in mind the fact that trades don't necessarily need to be financial. They can take place as simple as legal contractsor auditing consumer products and data storage.

Blockchain is essentially a massive database that isn't stored in a central place. A floating database, if you will. Since it's not kept in one location, the transactions made by the blockchain can be made publicly accessible and observable. It is back to the concept of decentralization and not having to depend on one individual or government to guarantee the security of our transactions.

More concretely, think about it as if all your financial records were stored in one spreadsheet. Not very secure, would you say? Even if you had offline and online backups, those are just two or three possible points for failure. Blockchain allows the spreadsheet to be shared across many databases and constantly refreshed. This means that any changes made would be recorded, and there is no way for hackers to corrupt it at just one entry point because there is no single entry point and no singular point of failure.

Blockchain technology can transfer anything from crypto to tangible assets, such as property, without intermediaries such as banks or any other financial institution. It could save businesses and consumers billions each year, which is spent on transaction costs. While Bitcoin has received more media attention than the general public, blockchain technology has received more attention from businesses.

BLOCKCHAIN REFER TOBITCOIN and CRYPTOCURRENCY?

Bitcoin cannot be considered a blockchain, and blockchain isn't Bitcoin as well as any other cryptocurrency. Bitcoins and other cryptocurrencies are exchanged on a publicly accessible network with blockchain tech.

Blockchain is the technology that facilitates Bitcoin along with other crypto transactions. However, as we've already mentioned, blockchain technology has many other potential applications. It is possible to think of blockchain as an operating system as well as Bitcoin is of the many applications that operate on the system.

Bitcoin or Cryptocurrency Drawbacks

Insufficient Financial Regulation and the ability to Fund Black Market Activity

One of the significant advantages of cryptocurrency is an area of weakness. Their anonymity makes them a perfect tool for large-scale black market operations and their use for money laundering. For instance, Silk Road - an underground dark net marketplace, acted as an illegal black market for drugs. The transactions were conducted in Bitcoin to guarantee the anonymity of sellers and buyers. The website was closed in 2013 after raking in around

$1.2billion in revenues. Its founder Ross William Ulbricht was convicted of eight charges and sentenced to life in prison.

Another unsavoury use for cryptocurrency is ransomware. Ransomware is the term used to describe malicious software that hackers download onto the user's computer and then require payments in Bitcoin to break the software, allowing the user to access their data in the future. Ransomware has gained popularity because of the use of cryptocurrency as a form of payment. It means that the perpetrators behind the attacks can receive their ransom without revealing their identities.

Hackers

The biggest issue about cryptocurrency, as with any technology in its initial stages (which cryptocurrency is), will likely be security flaws. Hackers are responsible for several of the most significant dips in the market for cryptocurrency.

Tokyo Japan Bitcoin Exchange Mt. Gox had suffered losses of up to $27.2 million, while users lost around $460 million worth of Bitcoin when the exchange was compromised in 2011. In the year, it was the biggest cryptocurrency exchange in the world. Earth. Amid rumours of poor management and inadequate security procedures, The business eventually went bankrupt due to the hacking scandal.

Bitfinex, a Hong Kong-based exchange that was attacked in 2016, and customers lost around $72 million in Bitcoin.

It is vital to understand that hacking attacks involving Bitcoin or other cryptocurrencies were carried out at the level of exchange or wallet and not at the technological level. For more information about how to secure your cryptocurrency, go to the section on wallets in this book.

Human error and data loss If they are appropriately secured, cryptocurrencies can facilitate the change away from money that could degrade and diminish in time. Since the data is secured and stored on the internet, no person (bar hackers) can access your money.

But, this assumption requires a perfect level of accountability from the user. As you might have realized in the past, no one is perfect. Things get lost. For instance, we may lose encryption keys to our private accounts when they are stored on paper. Or, devices may be destroyed or taken using physical encryption wallets (like USB wallets).

The Speculation and the Misinformation

As we've mentioned, Bitcoin and cryptocurrencies are a new technological frontier. Therefore, the mainstream media, most of which don't employ professionals in this area, could likely disinformation about the technology and the market itself. In general, statements like "Bitcoin is more effective at being more valuable as opposed to gold" will not do anything but weaken the technology over the long term, but they are suitable for soundbites to mainstream media

In June 2017, the Ethereum market briefly crashed following unsubstantiated rumours by 4Chan, which claimed that the founder Vitalik Buterin was killed in a car crash. The hoax led to the market's value plummeting by $4 billion in less than 24 hours. This is a sign that the market's volatility generally is vulnerable to manipulation by unsavoury forces.

If you're considering trading in cryptocurrency, you should be prepared to endure rapid rises and drops in the market, which is much more volatile than conventional stocks. This is why being a wise trader will aid you greatly.

China

The relationship between China and cryptocurrency is unique from any other nation. The United States has been more instrumental in cryptocurrency's growth than the Middle Kingdom. Cryptocurrencies are a favourite for Chinese investors because of the government's strict regulations regarding their currency of choice, the Yuan. The most significant of these is the devaluation of their money, which has lowered its value in investments and trading.

This has resulted in many wealthy and less wealthy private individuals searching for new ways to increase their wealth. They are seen by many as more secure assets as compared to traditional investment options. China's abundance of energy at a low cost has been a significant source of the cryptocurrency mining market that is currently not accessible to the majority of people who are Western European or Americans. About 70% of the world's cryptocurrency mining market is in China.

China is also at risk of mass manipulation of information. Rumour-mongering, mistranslations, and coin pumping are more likely to exploit the Chinese market because of the absence of foreign media, particularly in cryptocurrency. In June 2017 and June 2017, the People's Bank of China (PBoC) stated in response to inaccurate reports claiming that its central bank gave cryptocurrency as a whole. The claims were believed to be part of a pyramid scheme designed to attract investors under the pretence of a cryptocurrency that a government backs.

Survivorship Bias & Gambler's Fallacy

Contrary to what find on online forums and social media. Some people lost money on cryptocurrency. It's just an issue of purchasing and selling at the incorrect timing.

This is why casinos continue to operate; winners boast to their family and friends while the losers remain secluded.

Be aware that you should never invest more money than you can afford to lose.

How to PurchaseCryptocurrency

There are two methods to purchase cryptocurrency, and the second is to utilize fiat currency (USD, EUR, GBP, etc.) to buy cryptocurrency using an exchange. Exchanges work similarly to traditional foreign currency exchanges. Prices fluctuate daily and, like other currency exchange markets, are available 24 hours a day. The businesses earn theirrevenue by charging a small amount for every transaction.

Some charge buyers and sellers, while others charge an amount for purchasing. To protect their customers, most ofthese exchanges will ask for verification of your identity before you can buy cryptocurrency.

It is essential to know the kind of payment that each exchange accepts. Certain businesses accept debit and credit card payments, whereas others accept PayPal or wire transfers from banks. Below are three of the most popular and reliable currency exchanges that allow you to purchase BitCoin, Ethereum, and other altcoins that use fiat currencies such as US dollars, Euros, and British Pounds.

Coinbase

The largest exchange of currency worldwide, Coinbase allows users to buy, sell, and store cryptocurrency. Coinbase is, without doubt, the most accessible exchange available to anyone who wants to join this market. Once your identity is verified, you can purchase cryptocurrency with a debit credit or debit card within a few minutes. They currently allow trading in BitCoin, Ethereum, and LiteCoin with fiat currencies. The exchange is known for its extraordinary security measures and policies concerning the storage of money. They also have an operational iPhone and Android app that allows trading and buying at the touch of a button, which is hugely beneficial if you're trying to trade.

If you sign-up for Coinbase by clicking this link, you'll receive $10 worth of Bitcoin following your first purchase that exceeds $100 of cryptocurrency.

Kraken

The company is located in Canada and is currently the most significant exchange by volume of Euro-based purchases. Kraken offers more support for a cryptocurrency (they allow for buying Monero, Ethereum Classic and Dogecoin) than Coinbase. They allow margin trading, which, though not the area of a novice, could be helpful to experienced traders.

For other cryptocurrencies like Dash and Golem, you will require access to an exchange that facilitates cryptocurrency-to-cryptocurrency trading. The most effective one is Poloniex.

Poloniex

With over 100 currencies available and data analysis for experienced traders, Poloniex is the complete exchange open. Its low trading costs are another benefit, and it's a fantastic location to trade your Bitcoin or Ethereum into another cryptocurrency. The most significant disadvantage to Poloniex is that it cannot accept deposits in fiat currencies, meaning you'll need to make your first Bitcoin or Ethereum purchases on Coinbase and Kraken.

Things to consider before investing in CRYPTOCURRENCY

Understanding all the technical aspects of cryptocurrency is not required before you invest. But, knowing the answers to a few basic questions can help you determine whether to put your money into a cryptocurrency or not. Here are some critical questions you must know the answers to before investing in the world of the coin.

- What is the issue that the coin attempt to address?

- How can the coin address this issue?

- What makes this coin's solution the most effective solution available? Do you think it's the best solution?

- Who is the group behind this coin? What is their history of development? What is their code's transparency? Are they open source?

- Is there a publicly-owned figurehead that will be accountable in the event of any issues regarding adoption or development?

- Is this coin have competitors' currencies? If so, what's the advantage of coin A over coin B?

Bitcoin (BTC)

At the date of writing: $4,070.13. It is available on

Fiat: Coinbase, Poloniex, Kraken

The coin that sparked the entire thing is now considered one of the world's greatest assets. Its market cap is more than

$67 billion, and the currency can be worth much more to corporations like PayPal. We've discussed Bitcoin in detail before, and this article will discuss it as a way to invest.

The price is currently at a whopping $4,000 for each coin; many experts have said that Bitcoin isn't feasible for ordinary investors; however, that's an opinion that I disagree with.

The first thing to remember is that it is crucial to keep in mind that cryptocurrency is not the same as ordinary stocks, as they can be divided. Therefore, if you'd like to put your money into Bitcoin, there is no need to buy the entire coin. You can purchase fractions of the currency, so even if you have only $100, you can start your journey in this market.

Additionally, the fact that Bitcoin is a type of "digital gold" continues to make it the most expensive cryptocurrency. This makes Bitcoin the perfect investment because the price of other currencies is correlated to Bitcoin.

Another reason any portfolio should have Bitcoin is that if you decide to purchase one of the less well-known cryptocurrencies, it is necessary to exchange them for Bitcoin instead of buying them directly in fiat currency.

Bitcoin Cash (BCH/BCC)

The price at the date of writing: is $326.77. Exchanges:

Fiat: Bitfinex, Kraken, Bithumb (ROK) ViaBTC (CN), Bter (CN), Huobi (CN), Bitcoin Indonesia (INR)

BTC: Bittrex, Poloniex, Cryptopia (NZ)

Bitcoin cash came into existence in the wake of an unintended break, known as the "hard fork" in the Bitcoin technology, on August 1, 2017. The ultimate goal Bitcoin Cash is pursuing is to function as a currency that can be usedworldwide.

The split resulted from issues with Bitcoin's capability to complete transactions at a fast speed. For instance, the Visanetwork can process approximately 1,700 transactions per second, whereas Bitcoin averages around 7. As the networkexpands, so do the waiting periods for transactions. BCC hopes to handle more transactions as well offering lower transaction costs.

One of the leading solutions to this problem is to increase the volume of each block to enable more data to be processed simultaneously. This will help solve the issue of scalability Bitcoin faced before. The technology could work in the near term, with the first Bitcoin Cash block recordingmore than 7,000 transactions, as opposed to Bitcoin's 2,500.

The outcome of the failure of Bitcoin Cash will mostly depend on the adoption by Bitcoin of SegWit's technology inthe coming year and its ability to handle transactions faster and to function as a currency instead of being a speculation- based asset. The detractors have expressed concerns regarding security with Bitcoin Cash.

A variety of cryptocurrency exchanges are extensively adopting Bitcoin Cash. At the time of writing, there are only a few weeks of data, and, as such, nobody has been capable of executing any long-term trends or technical analyses of BCH as an asset. If the adoption of BCH continues to grow, the price is expected to remain on the rise. Initial price increases for Bitcoin Cash were primarily caused by the demand of South Korea, with over 50 per cent of the overall trade volume coming from South Korean exchanges.

Mining companies have quickly embraced the currency because of its more significant mining ROI than Bitcoin. The lower difficulty of mining (leading to greater rewards from mining) will continue to increase the incentive for mining companies to shift their funds from Bitcoin to Bitcoin Cash.

Note: Depending on the trading partner, Bitcoin Cash may use the symbol BCC or BCH Double-check before making a trade

Ethereum (ETH)

Prices at the date at the time of this writing ($225.07) Available at:

Most significant exchanges allow the purchase of Ethereum in exchange for fiat currency and also exchange it for BTC

If Bitcoin held the lead in the cryptocurrency market between 2008 and 2016, 2017 is Ethereum's year. The relatively new cryptocurrency has already made an impression on the market by introducing some incredible technological advancements which could be ground- breaking and even game-changing.

It is important to note that Ethereum isn't an actual cryptocurrency but an exchange that uses blockchain technology. However, tokens referred to as "ether" can be traded on numerous exchanges. They can be utilized to pay for transactions via the Ethereum blockchain or sold with other currencies or cash. Many online articles use the words "Ethereum" or "Ether" interchangeably.

The area where Ethereum excels is in its new technology called "smart contracts." Some have referred to it as a technology that can replace accountants and lawyers. They are programmable contracts made using blockchain technology that can be programmed to run automatically when certain conditions are fulfilled. For instance, an automated transfer of 10 ethers could be made into the person's wallet after person A has completed a task to person B. Person B has no chance to break this contract once the conditions are met, as the blockchain enforces the termsof the contract.

The possibilities for smart contracts are endless. From managing to government and even being able to create an auto-executing could, that is a fantastic technology. Many of the most significant international banks have set up thought-tanks for technology similar to this, and the adoption of every major institution has the possibility of sending Ethereum's price to the heights. It is believed that the Blockchain Banking Consortium project involves 43 banks worldwide and seeks to establish a blockchain-basednetwork that will enable the large-scale international transfer of funds.

The platform is in its development phase, and there are onlysome real-world examples of large-scale Ethereum Blockchain implementation today. But many investors believe in the technology. This plays majorly in explaining the price increase throughout 2017. In just a month, from May 18 to June, 12the price increased from $96.65 to a highof $395.03.

Ethereum has also experienced the loss of $4 billion in a single day in market capitalization following a hoax rumourconcerning the death of the founder Vitalik Buterin gained traction after appearing on the message board 4Chan. Let this be another cautionary tale: cryptocurrency is more vulnerable to market manipulation than traditional investments.

Ripple (XRP)

Price at the Time of Writing $0.15 $0.15 Price available:Fiat: Bitstamp, GateHub

BTC: Poloniex, Bittrex, Kraken, Coincheck (JP), Bitso(MEX), Coinone (ROK)

The third-largest cryptocurrency in market capitalization remains under the radar of many journalists and investors. In 2012, it was first introduced and acts as a payment platform, and a protocol Ripple intends to provide "secure quick, fast and virtually free global payments." Ripple transactions are currently processed in less than 4 seconds. The platform's ultimate goal is to render obsolete payment platforms with lengthy transaction times and costly charges like SWIFT and Western Union bygone.

Many global banks use Ripple's payment platform, which includes majors like BBVA, Bank of America, and UBS. By using Ripple's payment system, banks can convert currency in a single step, even for nations that aren't well-known, and money like a change from Albanian Lek into Vietnamese Dong. This could also reduce the requirement to use intermediary currencies, such as US euro or euros. As per Ripple, switching to the platform could reduce banks' costs by, on average, $3.76.

With the growing acceptance of the world's banking industry, Ripple is off to an excellent beginning, particularly if you view it as you would an established start-up.

Ripple is also the most amount of coins (known by the name XRP) accessible from any currency, with 100 billion (39 billion) available to the general public). In contrast, Bitcoin is only 16 million coins, and Ethereum is 94 million. In contrast to many open-source cryptocurrencies, The source code for Ripple is owned by a private company. The 100 billion coins available are also "unstained" It is possible that the owners can produce more at any moment, reducing the value of any currency held. The central ownership of the coins is at odds and those who think cryptocurrency can be used as a weapon against only one owner. Researchers from Purdue University also determined that the platform has "security issues," but at the time of writing, there were no significant incidents involving the venue.

Dash (DASH)

Prices at the date when this article was written: $194.25. Onsale:

Fiat: Bitfinex, xBTCe, Bithumb (ROK), BTC: Poloniex, Bittrex

Kraken

The term "digital cash" is short for "digital cash." Dash concentrates on the speed of transactions and privacy as its two principal selling points. Before its name, Darkcoin and later rebranded to separate itself from the "dark web" of illicit cryptocurrency. Dash is focused on security, usability, and the market for consumers. The cryptocurrency is currently between the top 5 and 8 largest cryptocurrencies in market capitalization.

By speeding up the processing speed using Bitcoin through its Masternode network, transactions are almost instantaneous compared to the 10-minute waiting time in Bitcoin transactions. Users must deposit a minimum of 1000 DASH to become a controller node. This led to a disagreement over whether DASH is truly a cryptocurrency that is decentralized or it is not.

Dash is not as liquid as Bitcoin, so you'll be unable to complete large-scale orders. However, Dash is being adopted by more exchanges each month. Dash's growth potential depends on its access and acceptance by the general market. One example is Breitbart, an Irish discount gift card site that provides customers up to a 20% discount on Amazon purchases when they pay with Dash.

Another area where Dash can be used is the current Venezuelan crisis with currency. Venezuelan cryptocurrency exchange CryptoBuyer has begun offering Dash instead of the national Bolivar currency that was and continues to suffer from hyperinflation. Venezuelans are looking to protect their savings, and cryptocurrencies such as Dash permit them to accomplish this by storing worth against USD. US dollar.

Another thing to note is that the most affluent 10 DASH holders have 10.1 per cent of the coin's total value, nearly double the amount for Bitcoin and Bitcoin Cash.

It could be a problem if one of these big players influences market developments.

Monero (XMR)

The price at the date at the time of publishing: $43.22. Available on:

Fiat: Kraken, HitBTC, Bter (CN)

BTC: Poloniex, Bitfinex, Bittrex, Bitsquare

Monero lets users transfer and receives money without needing a public transaction record through the cryptocurrency blockchain. The majority of Monero transactions are encrypted by default. If you value the privacy of your customers first, then Monero is a perfect fit. Monero was designed to be private and not traceable. This is evident in the development team that, unlike other coins, does not have a public CEO or persona.

Monero also uses "ring signatures, " a particular kind of cryptography that guarantees non-traceable transactions. It allows users to transfer cash but not be able to connect the address directly to their sender. This can be viewed as either positive or negative, depending on your perspective about privacy. Ring signatures can also hide the number of transactions and the identities of the seller and buyer. In contrast to

Dash, Monero has been open source since the beginning, meaning anyone can access the program's code to ensure total transparency.

The security of the currency can make it preferred for dark- web users. Before it was shut down, the market on the darknet AlphaBay had embraced Monero and BitCoin for processing transactions. Everything from illegal drugs to weapons or stolen credit cards is traded through the platform. Monero's anonymity has also resulted in Monero being the most sought-after venue for hackers who use ransomware.

It is yet to be determined whether Monero expands into more legitimate uses, for instance, to hide one's actual net worth. It is also unclear whether it will remain the preferred coin for more illegal industries to prevent the widespread adoption of other currencies. This uncertainty can be used to advantage speculators when they try to reap profits from the possibility of mass adoption.

Litecoin (LTC)

Price at the time of Writing $40.11 Fiat: Coinbase, Poloniex

BTC Exchanges: Most exchanges support BTC to LTC transactions.

The first altcoin Litecoin has been a non-flashy but steady growth in an industry fueled by hype and colossal boom and bust cycles. Due to this, some analysts have called it to be the "low risks coin." The coin was launched in 2011 to be "silver in comparison to the gold of Bitcoin" and fix the flaws that Bitcoin faced in the past. The limit on coins for Litecoin is four times Bitcoin's limit at 84 million coins. This makes it an inflationary currency. The time required to create blocks is 2.5 minutes, which is about a quarter of Bitcoin's time of 10 minutes. Litecoin was the longest-running second most popular cryptocurrency according to market capitalization before the growth of Ethereum in 2017.

The ability of Litecoin to process more transactions because of its speedy block generation provides it with a distinct benefit over Bitcoin. Merchants can send and receive payments almost immediately with no transaction cost. Bitcoin is the opposite. It could take four times as long to make the same transaction and with a more significantprice. Litecoin is also one of the fastest development teams of all cryptocurrencies, allowing it to undergo regular and cutting-edge improvements, such as being the first cryptocurrency to implement Segregated Witness (SegWit) technology. This gives the coin an advantage because it is the world's second-most secure blockchain, following Bitcoin.

Another advantage for prospective investors is the increased use of significant exchanges. Most major cryptocurrency exchanges accepted Litecoin transactions in fiat currency like Coinbase in March of 2017, which was a huge benefit, especially for US and EU investors. Regarding market behaviour, Bitcoin and Litecoin follow the same pattern of increases and decreases in value. Many investors opt for Litecoin as a second option in addition to Bitcoin to diversify their portfolios.

Litecoin's system is significantly more straightforward if you are interested in mining, reducing mining expenses and entry barriers.

Litecoin uses the Scrypt algorithm, whereas Bitcoin is based on SHA-256. The primary benefit of this is that it has a lower cost for mining since Scrypt is not as demanding as Graphic Processing Units (GPUs). In 2017 Bitcoin mining has become an attractive alternative for the beginner or home-based miner; however, Litecoin mining is still able to turn profits, even after considering electricity costs in the first world nations.

Some of Litecoin's opponents have criticized the cryptocurrency as "just another Bitcoin that has no originality." It was also the victim of a Chinese scam in 2015 where investors collected 22% of all coins before throwing them.

Factom (FCT)

The price at the time of writing is $19.71

Fiat: Coincheck (JP), Yuanbao (CN), BTC: Poloniex, Bittrex

Like Ethereum, Factom expands on ways to utilize blockchain technology that isn't limited to currency. In contrast, Ethereum is built on two-way verification and ensures that contracts are indestructible. Factom promises to accomplish the same feat with massive data blocks by providing records that cannot be altered. This will allow companies and government agencies to keep a record of information without losing or changing it. The possible applications include legal documents, company accounts, medical records, and voting systems. Imagine a world in which it would be physically impossible to fake the results of an election or that an accounting scandal similar to Enronwould never occur again.

Like other blockchain projects, Factom cannot be altered because no one runs the network. The network is controlled by millions of people in complete isolation from each other. Although data belonging to one individual is susceptible to hacking, maliciousness, user error, and alteration, this is not feasible with the data belonging to the whole network.

In terms of investing, similar to what Ether can be about Ethereum, Factoids are the "currency" of the Factom system. The more applications created by Factom, the greater Factoids are worth.

Factom has already signed an agreement with consultancy firm iSoftStone to offer blockchain-based management software to cities in China. The deal includes plans to provide auditing and verification services.

Factom Chief Executive Officer Peter Kirby described the technology: "We believe this will enable developers to develop a new category of secure and accountable business systems. It could be used in financial services, insurance medical records, real estate - any area where record-keeping is crucial."

As with other commonly asked blockchain technologies, Factom is the scale and greater technology acceptance. The main issue with Factom investing is whether the company can manage the system to an unbeatable profit over time or if the technology could be a race towards the bottom of cost.

Neo (NEO)

Prices at the Time of Writing Price at the Time of Writing

$7.89. It is available on

Fiat: Yunbi (CN), Jubi (CN) BTC: Bittrex, Binance

One of the first Chinese blockchain projects based in China, Neo, formerly known as Antshares, is proud to be open source and community-driven. It has been similar to Ethereum in that it has smart contracts rather than acting as a token that functions like Bitcoin. The project was created by ONCHAIN, a Shanghai firm based in China known as ONCHAIN.

In a press conference at Microsoft's Microsoft China HQ in Beijing Beijing, Antshares CEO Da Hongfei revealed the brand's rebranding as Neo and some projects currently in the pipeline. The announcements included collaboration with the certificate officials in China to track real-world assets with smart contracts.

Neo's location in China gives it access to China's second largest and most significant cryptocurrency market, which could be seen as a distinct advantage compared to other cryptocurrencies. However, the downsides currently are the limited availability of wallets that can be used for the cryptocurrency itself.

At the event, Srikanth Raju, GM, Developer Experience & Evangelism and Chief Evangelist for the Greater China Region, Microsoft declared the ONCHAIN was "one of the most prestigious 50 startups within China." Its support and positive publicity from a powerful world-class company such as Microsoft will only be positive for Neo in the future.

Perhaps the most critical determinant in the direction of NEO in the future is backing from the Chinese government. While other cryptocurrency types face legal battles with governments, Neo's relationship with Chinese management has been less than but somewhat positive; Da Hongfei, the founder, has been a frequent participant in the government's conferences and seminars on blockchain and cryptocurrency.

A thing to be cautious of is that Neo is, once more, it's a Chinese aspect. This time, it's the language barrier. Most of the information about Neo is reported in Chinese at the beginning, which means there's an opportunity for mistranslations within the English-spoken world. For instance, "partnerships" with Microsoft and Alibaba (China's largest company in eCommerce) are overhyped because of the poor translations from Chinese media sources. However, this doesn't mean that collaborations like this won't be possible in the future.

The smart contracts on Antshares cover equity, creditor claims, bills, and currencies.

Update to July 2017. NEO trades at $51.99. In just two weeks, the price jumped by more than 500 per cent

Golem (GNT)

Price as of the date of writing: $0.26 It is available on: Fiat: Yunbi

(CN)

BTC: Poloniex, Bittrex, Liqui

Golen is a cryptocurrency that is based upon Ethereum Blockchain technology. Some commentators have described it as the "Airbnb for computing" The coin's worth is built around the software that could be created with it.

The people who founded the Golem Project describe it as a "supercomputer" that can connect with other computers to accomplish various tasks. This includes scientific research data analysis, data analysis, and mining cryptocurrency. For instance, if your computer is not using power, by using it on the Golem system, you could rent the energy (hence that AirBNB analogy) to another person who needs it. The person who needs the additional power can gain access to supercomputer-like processing power at only a fraction of the cost of having the capability to process.

The possibility that users can earn cash from the power they don't use is. Theoretically, it's a simple concept, but what isn't yet clear is the application in the practice of this technology. The Golem team's lack of visibility has also hurt the value of the coin in the recent past. The inability to purchase GNT using fiat currency (such as USD) is another disadvantage for those buying on the mass market.

It is important to note that the technology for the project is in its early stage of development, and as of August 17, 2017, they are still searching for beta testers. It is believed that the Golem Project has a very likely chance of going into nothing. On the other hand, there's an excellent chance for huge future gains, even if a coin costs less than $0.30.

(STEEM)

The price at the date of writing: is $1.10. It is available on

Fiat: OpenLedgerDEX (Eur) BTC: Poloniex, Bittrex

Steam is one of the most exciting cryptocurrencies on the market right now. Steam is the currency built into the platform of social networking Steemit. Users can publish content, such as blog posts or long articles. This content is paid for in the format of digital coins. Like Reddit users earn upvotes, Steemit users are rewarded with Steem tokens, also known as Steem Dollars.

The financial incentive helps ensure that users work hard to produce high-quality content. The platform permits posts covering various topics, from cryptocurrency discussions to sports news and poetry.

Steem dollars are about $1 at the moment's exchange rate. They must be converted into Steem for exchange into fiat currencies or cryptocurrency. This is because they could be compared against the worth of the US dollar to limit the possibility of inflation decreasing their value. Steemit goes even further and offers users the option of earning 10% interest for any Steem dollars they hold in their account for over a year.

The biggest drawback is that the currency's success depends on the website's overall performance. Suppose the site reaches the point of no return and the coin's value. Some have questioned the Steemit platform's credibility and whether it could be an enormous pump and dump or an elaborate pyramid scheme. The argument stems from the fact that many of the most popular posts were promoting the Steemit platform. There have been concerns due to automated bots that steal content to get additional votes.

The website's creators have responded to criticism with a statement that they have specific security measures to keep the content updated and provide users with an additional incentive to keep their Steem coins. Their method of doing this is via a technique called Steem Power. Steem Power is a way for users to secure their money for the long-term by investing them directly into the platform. When they convert Steem into Steem Power, users have an increased weighting of votes on the forum. They also change into "power users," without a better word.

The main advantage Steem has over other cryptocurrencies is that it is the most specific cryptocurrency to use with no expenditure due to its design. Instead of buying coins from an exchange or paying for computers and equipment to mine the coins, users can sign up on the site to get a free account and start publishing content to earn cash. It's the most affordable hurdle in the entryway for every currency on the market for cryptocurrency. While making substantial gains can be challenging at first, some users have earned thousands of dollars of Steem with just a single post.

IOTA (MIATA)

Time at the Price of Writing Time at the Price of Writing

$0.92 The price is on sale onFiat: Bitfinex BTC: Bitfinex

IOTA is the boringly name Internet of Things (IoT). The coin is a second cryptocurrency based on blockchain technology; however, it has an added twist.

The IOTA team behind IOTA is placing the future of IOTA on a concept called Tangle, a new technology in development that can be described as a blockchain that does not require blocks. If Tangle succeeds, the entire network could be distributed. This could result in ZERO problems with scalability, which every other cryptocurrency faces. If this technology works, this could prove to be a total game changer in the cryptocurrency market. Imagine a world free of mediators, and imagine the huge savings in costs that could be achieved.

The fundamental idea of the currency is that it has a near- zero cost of transactions, even for transfers of tiny quantities of money. It's something that no other currency or technology can promise at the moment or even giants such as Bitcoin and Ethereum. With a focus on available micro or nano transactions, there are numerous applications for both businesses and consumers' technological solutions for financial transactions. The technology is open-source, meaning anyone can access the source code and keep track of the evolution of the currency should you be so inclined.

The reason for the low value of the cryptocurrency in its current state is that the technology is only conceptual. The issues that affect the entire cryptocurrency industry, such as widespread adoption and security, must be addressed.

The issue must be addressed before the coin can move on to the next step. The team behind the development has numerous issues to resolve regarding the creation of technology, not even the marketing.

Dogecoin (DOGE)

Price as of the date of publication: $0.0019 Price available: Fiat: YoBit, BTC38 (CN)

BTC: HitBTC, Poloniex, Bittrex

A meme that came to be having actual worth. The most popular among Shiba Inus around the world The dogecoin concept was invented by Jackson Palmer in 2013 and was a trend in cryptocurrency.

The value of Dogecoin is primarily derived from an internet- based form, "tipping." One of the most famous examples is when holders offer dogecoins to Reddit users in exchange for comments they liked. Dogecoin ended up becoming one of the two highest "tipped" cryptocurrencies following Bitcoin as the demand for Dogecoin reached a height of A

$60 million market cap was announced in the early part of the year 2014. The campaign to take the Jamaican Bobsled team to the Winter Olympics was partly funded through the coin. $25,000 was donated to the UK charitable service dog.

The coin erupted simultaneously as it rose following the Dogecoin exchange. Moolah declared bankruptcy. The CEO, Ryan Kennedy, aka

Alex Green/Ryan Gentle, was sentenced to eleven years in prison for allegations of sexual harassment. Kennedy was believed to have caused between

$2 and 4 million in losses for those who contributed to the project.

The current status of the coin remains that of a relaxed, enjoyable community-based project which rewards forum posts. Dogecoin remains one of the largest and most actively-active communities among all cryptocurrencies. Its supporters are hopeful that one day it will regain its status among the Internet's most popular cryptocurrencies.

Where to store your crypto Cold Storage and Wallets

If you've succeeded in purchasing a cryptocurrency, whether it's Bitcoin, Ethereum, or another altcoin, You'll require a place to keep it safe.

The cryptocurrency wallet is similar to a traditional bank account in that you can use it to make purchases and see the exact amount of cash you have. But, cryptocurrency wallets differ from traditional currency wallets due to the nature of the technology used to create the coins; for those who don't know that the way technology functions means that your currency isn't kept in a single central place. It's marked on the blockchain. This is why there is a public record of each coin's ownership; when a transaction is made; the document changes.

You can keep crypto in your purchased exchange, such as Coinbase or Poloniex. It is recommended not to do so for several reasons.

1.   Like all online entities exchanges, these are susceptible to attack, regardless of their security level or the measures they implement. This was the case in the Mt. Gox exchange in June 2011.

2.   Your passwords for these exchanges are susceptible to trojan horses, keyloggers, and other computer virus programs.

3.   You may accidentally create a login using an untrusted service such as coinbose.com (example) rather than coinbase.com

Cold storage is a system that allows you to take the cryptocurrency off. They include offline wallets made of paper physical bearer products like Bitcoin in physical formor a USB drive. We will discuss the advantages and disadvantages of each.

The cryptocurrency wallets come with two keys. One is public, and the other an individual one. These are represented using long characters. For example, a public keycould be

02a1633cafcc01ebfb6d78e39f687a1f0995c62fc95f51ead10a 02ee0be551b5dc -or it could be shown as a QR code. Publickeys are the account you use to accept cryptocurrency from others. It is completely secure to share the public keys with any person. Anyone with access to your public key will onlybe able to make deposits into your account.

However, your private key allows you to transfer cryptocurrency to other people. Every transaction is based on the recipient's and sender's private keys.

It is recommended to keep an off-site backup copy of your keys if the hardware fails and data is lost. If someone has access to your private key, they can withdraw money from your account. This is the first rule in cryptocurrency storage.

The most important rule for storing cryptocurrencies is never to share your private keys with anyone. Ever.

Paper Wallets:

Paper wallets are notepads of your keys that you write down on paper. They usually have QR codes that can be quickly scanned by the person sending them to transfer cryptocurrency.

Pros:

* Cheap

Your private keys aren't stored in a digital format; thus, they are safe from cyber-attacks and hardware malfunctions.

Cons:

* Paper loss because of human error

* Paper is brittle and may rapidly degrade in specific environments.

It is not easy to pay for bitcoin quickly; if you need to, it is not suitable for day-to-day transactions

Recommendations:

It is recommended to keep your wallet's paper in a bag sealed with plastic to shield it from water or humid conditions. If you're holding cryptocurrency over the long term, keep the wallet secure.

Be sure to read and comprehend the step-by-step guidelines before printing any wallets made of paper.

Bitcoin: http://bitaddress.org http://bitcoinpaperwallet.com Ethereum: http://myetherwallet.com/Litecoin:

https://liteaddress.org/

Look up a trusted cryptocurrency forum for all other currencies to get the most current suggestions on paper andoffline storage wallets.

Hardware Wallets

Hardware wallets refer to physical storage devices that hold your private keys. The most commonly used form of them has secured USB sticks.

The wallets are designed to use two-factor authentication, also known as 2FA, to ensure that only the wallet owner can access the information. For instance, one factor can be the USB stick you plug into your computer. The alternative is a four-number pin code, much as you would use a debit card to take money out of an ATM.

Pros:

* Nearly impossible to hack at the time of writing, there have occurred ZERO instances of hacking hardware wallets

If a virus or malware infects your computer, your wallet is not accessible because of 2FA

This remote code is never left on your device nor transferred to a computer. Therefore, yet again, malware or computers infected aren't an issue.

* You can carry it around at a moment's notice should you require to spend your crypto

It is easier to make transactions using traditional paper wallets

* It is possible to store several addresses in one device

* For the gadget-lovers of your life, they're more attractive than a piece of paper

Cons:

* Costs more than paper wallets, starting at $60

* Easily damaged by hardware degradation, changes, and modifications in technology

* Different wallets work with different currencies

* Entrusting the service provider to provide a wallet that is not in use. Utilizing a second-hand

The wallet can be a significant security risk. Make sure you purchase your hardware wallet from reputable sources.

The most well-known of these are Trezor as well as Ledger wallets. For other altcoins not accepted by these wallets, you can make your own secure USB money-saving device by following the online instructions.

CRYPTOCURRENCY INVESTMENT MINDSET

FOMO and FUD are Two Terms to be cautious of

In the world of cryptocurrency, FOMO and FUD are among the most dangerous terms in the investor's vocabulary. These aren't exactly the most recent hotshot cryptocurrency coming from China; They are merely terms that've cost ignorant investors and traders money.

FOMO - Fear of Not Being able to Access

Fear of missing out leads individuals to invest excessively and put money into coins without doing their investigation or diligence. If you look on forums for cryptocurrency, you'll see hundreds of posts by people who are new to the market and asking for advice on what coins to purchase. Every day, there's a new, shiny thing that is being hyped by people, which causes less experienced investors to throw cash at it. This can lead to investors purchasing coins at the peak and then panicking about and selling the value falls just a few days later.

You must remember that you will not be able to win with any investment. You'll be unable to buy every coin right now, and others will make cash where you won't. Evaluating yourself only against yourself and reviewing your income and loss sheet is essential. Before investing in a coin, you should take the time to consider why you're deciding to invest in it and then re-examine the basic principles of the currency.

The fear of losing out on massive returns is a regular occurrence and is something nearly everyone suffers from. The best way to fight anxiety is to learn about blockchain technology and study each coin in detail before investing. When you make intelligent, well-thought investments, you will have a greater chance of gaining long-run earnings.

FUD Fear, Uncertainty, and Doubt

Incredulity, fear, and doubt are nothing to deter investors from trusting in cryptocurrency or its use. This could range from the spread of false information (such as the false Vitalik Buterin death reports) and stories that deny the real- world applications of cryptocurrency technology.

Certain cryptocurrency criminals have employed FUD to promote their agendas while hindering other currencies' growth. This is why it's essential to distinguish between rational critique or analysis of money. FUD. The more educated you're, the easier it is to discern the difference.

The source you get the news from is a different element. The social media industry is the source of FUD. Go to any crypto-related forum on Facebook or view videos on YouTube from one of the more popular channels, and you'll find people spreading FUD over every video. Instead, look for more critical crypto news sites less prone to FUD and ensure you get your information from multiple sources.

Gains from a short-term investment against. Long-terminvestments

The billionaire investment manager of hedge funds and crypto Michael Novogratz made a very excellent analogy when he compared the present situation of the market to the third innings of an MLB game. The market is active, and there are a variety of long- and short-term events that couldimpact the currency's value.

In contrast to the whole stock market, the cryptocurrency market operates 24/7/365. There is no time lag between public news or market reaction. There is never a dead moment.

If you are convinced of currencies' science, these dollars make sense as a long-term investment. For many of them, the time in the market can beat the market. This is where our second acronym originates.

HODL"Hold On" (For) the Good Life

A backronym is an abbreviation of "hold" focused on holding onto your currency in the event of a market down.

A lighter explanation is provided by Bitcointalk forum member "GameKyuubi," who inadvertently created the term "cryptocurrency" during a night of intoxication in 2013. (author's note: Don't buy or trade cryptocurrencywhen you are under the influence)

" What's the reason I'm holding? I'll explain the cause. It's because I'm not a good trader. I know that I'm a poor trader.

I could have sold a few seconds before each sale and purchased moments before every purchase, but nobody is soastonishing as you. "

You will experience market declines for any long-term investment - it's just how capitalism works. If you're in a rush to sell whenever you notice an even slight drop (and in the case of cryptocurrency, that's likely to happen a lot), If you do this, you're an easy way of losing cash in the long term.

The practice of HODL'ing has risks, too, as more and more coins are being introduced to the market - some won't remain at a high value. It's possible to compare it to the traditional stock market, including blue chip and penny stocks. The fact that a penny stock or tiny market-cap cryptocurrency trading at $0.08 doesn't mean it can grow for a long time. If the cryptocurrency's people or company fail to fulfil their commitments to the marketplace, the coin's value will fall and eventually become outdated.

Recall that hindsight can be easy. Making predictions about market fluctuations in a market like cryptocurrencies, which is as volatile, isn't. Be cautious when investing and do your investigation.

Paper profits in comparison to. Actual profits

Remember that until you've completed the sale of those coins, any profits you earn are only on paper. Since the cryptocurrency market is highly volatile, profit margins can change dramatically daily or even hourly. I advise you to take advantage of intermediate profits when you invest. You accomplish this by selling the majority of your portfolio at a profit.

As an example, if you purchase 100 dollars for one coin, one month later, the value of the coin has increased to $150. If you exchange 75 cents worth of the currency at

$150, you'll have 0.5 coins worth $75 on paper and an additional $75 in hard, cold cash. Making money for yourself is a smart strategy and one you should be doing if seeking to earn consistent income.

The opposite of this is not to sell when the market is down. If you adhered to the first rule of investing, which was never to invest more money than you can manage to risk, you don't have any reason to profit from selling your stock. You may read frightening headlines such as "Ethereum drops 40 percent" and "Litecoin is in a crash" However, in the long run, the majority of these coins will return to their prior levels or even higher. If you sell the currency at a loss, your cash will be gone forever.

The Chaincoin Pump and Dump Scheme - The Reasons to Be a thorough researcher before purchasing

This is an example of intelligent investing and how you obtain your data.

Chain coin (CHC) is a cryptocurrency that experienced an explosive price hike from $0.05 to nearly $6 in just a few days. Before that, it was accessible on two tinycryptocurrency exchanges and achieved a meagre trading volume. Its official Github (programming community) and Twitter accounts were down for several months before this, and only a few technological milestones had been achieved.

However, a YouTube channel called HighOnCoins began to promote the cryptocurrency heavily. Videos titled "Buy ChainCoin CHC" were posted within the channel. The track also advised users to create controller nodes (which needed 1,000 CHC). The way also encouraged users to purchase and keep the coins for a long time instead of trading them out to make profits. The idea is that if all invested in and saved the cash, the price would rise and increase.

However, Chaincoin was plagued by many fundamental flaws that included:

* There is no differentiation between other coins. Lack of innovation from developers

* Zero-real-world applications in comparison to other coins

The initial surge in investment created a stir within the crypto community. There were mixed reactions, ranging from disbelief by investors focused on the coin's fundamentals to excitement among ignorant people who believed that the coins were part of a getting wealthy quick plan.

The coin hit a record high of $6.81 on the 14th of July, 2017, just a few days after,

The coin's developers re-visited its GitHub page to make some minor tweaks. After a couple of days, the currency's value fell to $1. HighOnCoins said this was an attack by hackers, but exchange activity revealed several traders' massive loss of coins.

The chain coin is currently trading at $0.32.

GitHub Blog Store of Value summarized the incident: "This was a clear shift of money from the ignorant to the criminal." This is a warning not to invest in a coin based on the hype. Instead, support is based on confidence and a belief in the tech.

I'm sure you've discovered a wealth of information about cryptocurrency and how you can make money from trading or investing in these currencies. There are many aspects to consider when investing in cryptocurrency, and you can use these to determine a suitable investing and trading plan.

You might want to revisit this information several times and then decide what you're looking for in your relationship with the cryptocurrency market.

Then, determine how you'll go about reaching your objectives. Select the cryptocurrency exchange you want to use and where you'll keep your assets before investing in anyor more coins.

It is then time to determine how much you'll invest in each coin.

Keep in mind that diversity is crucial, and you shouldn't keep all of your holdings for the long run in one currency.

If you plan to invest in cryptocurrency, make sure you do it using Dollar cost averaging. This means that you don't purchase all your coins at once; instead, you are buying a set amount each month, week, or every day of the year. This means you won't be tied to a specific price but instead spread your investments, making them less susceptible to price fluctuations.

Make your trades rationally, not emotionally. If you are planning to hold cryptocurrency for the long haul, don't check the charts every few hours, or else you'll be mad. Changes are swift in the cryptocurrency market. Therefore, you must stay up to date with cryptocurrency developments and news. You could do this within less than 30 mins each day. Be sure to get information from many impartial sources.

Never decide to invest in a currency simply because "some person on the internet" advised you to.

What exactly is BLOCKCHAIN technology?

In the last few years, you've likely heard increasing numbers of people speaking about crypto and blockchain. If you're unsure about the terms you've listened to, don't worry, it's not a problem for everyone else. It's time to get on the blockchain bandwagon since blockchain technology is fast reaching the status of a consumer; with IBM estimates, 15% of banking institutions will have blockchain technology in place at the year's end.

Blockchain is the underlying technology that makes technology like cryptocurrency viable. In the most fundamental sense, it collects the most financial data at present and then replicates the data to a wide range of decentralized nodes that could be distributed worldwide. The process is not run through a centralized body or network but through a peer-to-peer system that utilizes digital signatures and cryptography to ensure everything runs efficiently.

Every block added to the chain has information about different transactions, perhaps the so-called smart contracts, and details that link it to other blocks surrounding it. The blocks are also stamped with time and aid the chain in determining its position within the chain. The transactions within each block are confirmed by block miners, a third party who is compensated for their efforts and then included in the chain.

Miners solve proof-of-work systems, meaning they have to solve complex mathematical problems using equipment designed to solve these. These equations protect against security breaches via the denial of attacks on service and keep the system running smoothly. The amount of compensation for this kind of work differs based on the cryptocurrency being mined and the number of people working on finishing the block they chose to mine. Many cryptocurrencies charge an amount for transactions which is a percentage of this fee paid to miners too.

Even though database data is scattered around the globe without central authority or certain parts of it are regularly examined by third organizations, the information stored on a blockchain is highly safe. This level of security does not result from an active attack against fraud but rather from the defence abilities of the method that blockchains are built.

If a transaction is transferred by a node that does not match what the other nodes are saying, the block is rejected to be replaced by an accurate one. In essence, for a fake block to get past the defences of the blockchain, it must appear on 51 per cent of the nodes within the system simultaneously. The complexity of this job means that it is possible to be achieved; however, the expense will far exceed the potential rewards of taking the initiative.

History lesson

To understand the real significance of blockchain technologies, it's essential to know its history. In 2008, a person, or some people under the name Satoshi Nakamoto published an idea in a whitepaper of the creation of a digital currency that could let people transfer money to one another in an anonymous manner. The paper, titled Bitcoin: A Peer to Peer Electronic Cash Systems, followed by the first bitcoin and blockchain code created under the same name. This code became available open-source, and the Nakamoto name was obliterated as developers started to work on it with a keen eye.

The Nakamoto pseudonym is also believed to be the first to distribute bitcoins and confirm the transaction, gaining 50 bitcoins as a reward. If you're considering investing in a cryptocurrency based on blockchain technologies, you should note that the first use for bitcoins was to exchange 10,000 bitcoins for two large pizzas worth around $.002. If you're not aware that they're doing much better than that, with each bitcoin valued at around September 2017, the amount was $5,000.

In 2014, blockchain use was beginning to gain momentum. A newly improved version of the code allowed complete programs to be stored in blocks, along with information enabling various tasks to be completed inside the blockchain. In 2016 in 2016, the Russian Federation started working on the blockchain to collect royalties from copyrighted materials and making Russia the first nation to launch a blockchain initiative; however, since then, several other countries, such as China along with the US, have stated that the possibility of working on blockchain-related projects that they have developed. In the project's announcement in 2016, it was reported that the Russian economic minister was quoted declaring that blockchain technology would be the most significant technological innovation since the advent of the internet.

Over the last couple of years, another blockchain-based business known as the Ethereum platform has been receiving lots of attention because of its broad range of capabilities that are superior to bitcoin's blockchain. The Ethereum platform comes with its currency, the ether (although both terms are frequently used interchangeably by some commentators). It also hosts an ecosystem of other coins that programmers have created to run within its framework. It also hosts many smart contracts and applications that run on "gas," a transaction fee collected by the platform for every transaction. Ether blocks that are mind-based are typically completed in shorter periods than bitcoin blocks. The Ethereum chain can handle many more blocks simultaneously compared to the bitcoin chain.

Differences in databases: The most significant distinction between blockchain-based databases and traditional ones is the degree of centralization required to allow them to run efficiently. Even though an ordinary server is decentralized, the elements will be placed in proximity as they can be to facilitate the exchange of data. Blockchains, however, are composed of nodes separated by miles, all communicating with each other via an optimal use model, which implies they naturally look for those nodes closest to them. The information is distributed from there.

The reality that mass collaboration and the blockchain code result in a secure method through which money can be transferred can be made. Blockchain is the very first digital medium through which value can be moved, much as the internet has allowed the transmission of information electronically.

Hash: A hash is a mathematical function that forms an essential component of the security matrix. The mechanism guarantees that data stored on a blockchain stays secure, regardless of who could gain access to it. The function encodes the data as a fixed-length output described as a form or digital fingerprint. Regarding blockchain security, the most widely employed hash function is SHA-256. Cryptocurrencies use SHA-256 like Bitcoin, Omni, and Zetacoin.

The hash function used for each block will be unique, meaning that if a malicious third party alters that data, the entire fingerprint will be rearranged in unpredictable ways. Additional information about the hash is added after blocks are added to the chain in their entirety. The process repeats every time the block is added to ensure that the blockchain constantly changes.

Merkle tree Hashes are used by a procedure known as the Merkle tree, a simple and quick way for blockchains to validate all their data after the new block is added. Every hash is distinct and is created according to the data it contains. The Merkle tree has to examine the soup and check it against the root hashes, which is the most comprehensive collection of all the soups. Then, it will check if everything matches precisely as it ought to. Every time the tree does that, it generates two root systems where the data is accurate. One that isn't, and this keeps the essential information of the blockchain secure from malicious alteration.

A PERSONAL APPLICATION FOR BLOCKCHAIN TECHNOLOGY

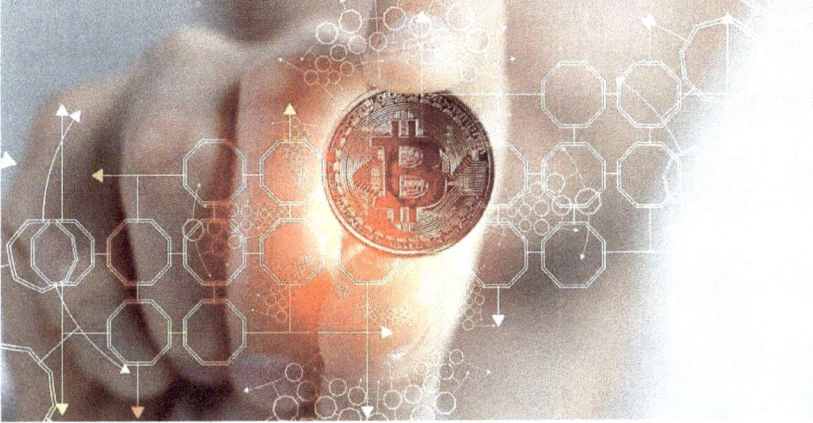

As blockchain technology continues to increase in popularity, the ways how it is put to usage are expanding as well. There are a variety of possible ways in which blockchain technology is likely to transform the way businesses are carried out, in day-to-day life, beyond the realm of cryptocurrency and the way that legislators and governments interact with the general public.

Uses for business

Transfers of money and payments Blockchain technology is already associated with cryptocurrency transactions; however, the reality to be said much more can be done in this space to meet better the needs of businesses in regards to using blockchain to its total capacity. The Ethereum Enterprise Alliance comprises a consortium of large corporations like Microsoft, JP Morgan, and Samsung. They are working to create a blockchain system based on Ethereum technology. Still, it also has the control level that businesses require to utilize the technology regularly.

Although extremely popular in some regions of the globe, this kind of service is complicated to find in other areas. This is why most people from Kenya are currently using an account with a bitcoin wallet then doing indoor plumbing. Connecting all new users with the Internet will likely have a significant positive impact on all retailers worldwide.

Notary service: Blockchain technology has been built to be utilized in place of traditional legal services. There are a variety of applications that permit the notarization of many kinds of content.

Cloud storage Blockchain technology has been utilized to connect users with cloud storage space in an Airbnb-like setup. With this system, those with extra room on their hard drives could lease out extra space to users needing additional storage. The estimates are that global cloud storage has amounted to more than $20 billion on cloud storage. This could be an opportunity to make money should this trend become popular.

In the case of fraud, Blockchain technology can enhance the efficiency of identifying identities online in a manner that is efficient and secure. Blockchain is the best option to address this issue because the results will be safely.

Secure, authenticated, unchangeable, and undisputed. The new system will eliminate complex passwords or dual authentication methods that require two factors for an approach that will utilize cryptography and digital signatures to ensure that everyone is secure and easily catalogued.

When using this type of technology, the transaction will be completed as usual. The only required test is that the account where the money is drawn matches that of the individual authorized the transaction. The same application of blockchain technology can also be employed in connection with birth certificates, passports, residency forms, passport accounts logins, or physical identity. Some available apps use blockchains to validate the user's identity from the mobile device.

Communication in the supply chain: If there is one aspect that businesses are having a difficult time with, it's the high amount of communication necessary to ensure that they have all needs in place to ensure that they are prepared to carry out whatever they need to do. Blockchain technology allows companies to track the progress of their products from door to door through the Internet of Things (the ability of everyday objects to transmit and receive information), connecting containers for shipping to accounts that receive a constant stream of information about the item in question when it reaches various thresholds, and then automatically pay for the items after they've got their destination. SkuChain and Provenance are two companies developing these kinds of systems.

Gift cards The gift card is great in theory but falls off in the real world when it's time for the recipient to use the gift card at issue. Blockchain technology can alter all that by linking customer loyalty products directly to a blockchain that can be used to verify and update the relevant information when needed. Gyft Block is a company with an electronic gift card that is up and running on bitcoin's blockchain. It can be traded as an actual cryptocurrency.

The Internet of Things: Samsung and IBM are currently working on a plan referred to by the name Autonomous decentralized peer-to-peer Telemetry or ADEPT uses blockchain to develop a system that blends the proof-of- stake and proof-of-work to more secure transactions. They're trying to create a system that acts as an open ledgerthat many different devices can use. The ledger's public nature will serve as a hub that could bridge between devices at the lowest cost. The devices would then be able to connect in a manner that is virtually autonomous and make it easierto conserve energy to fix bugs and push out updates.

Smart insurance contracts: They could revolutionize insurance in a significant way. Instead of dealing with insurance brokers who need to decide on liability in the event of a workplace-related accident, Blockchains would be able to take advantage of an intelligent contract that can issue the payment if an interconnected device detects a defective signal. Blockchain can then provide a more straightforward process for claiming that will improve the user experience and ultimately reduce the cost to the company.

Finance: 4G Capital is a business that offers access to creditto small-scale companies in Africa by using a decentralized application and operating on Ethereum. Ethereum blockchain. Users can use the app to pay money made in crypto directly with the person they wish to gift it to. The money is changed into an account in the country of the person who applied and distributed using a unique transfer system. Apart from providing 100 % unsecured loans to those who might not be able to obtain the funds otherwise, it offers business training and consultancy services. Although it is currently only in its infancy, other businesses that provide this financing will likely be created if it is successful.

Microblogging: Businesses are constantly searching for methods to connect with their customers, and blockchain might be the next technology. Projects such as Eth-Tweet provide decentralized microblogging services using the Ethereum blockchain. It functions similarly to Twitter, but it is a decentralized organization. There isn't anyone who can force users to delete content, and nobody can take down messages once they've become part of the network.

Day-to-Day Life

Healthcare: Real-world tests are being conducted to provide individuals with their healthcare status while they go through the hospital. The first studies by the MIT Media Lab show that this method can reduce errors by as much as 30 per cent in emergency circumstances. This is an enormous improvement for hospitals typically not built to handle the amount and variety of information generated today. Patients' data could be collected on an outpatient basis or if the patient has opted to join the test group. The payment for these tests can be made automatically after the necessary data is collected.

Internet decentralization: Since the growth of Google, the internet has become an increasingly centralized site than it was in the past. A company called Blockstack is trying to change everything about that. They plan to release a working prototype in the second quarter of 2017 that allows anyone to use blockchain technology to connect to the internet with better control of personal information. The decentralized internet will function like the traditional internet works, except that rather than creating a new account for each website, this process will be reversed, and you'll be able to establish a primary account, after which you will grant access to specific websites to it.

If you decide to stop with a particular site, you can take complete control of the access to your data at any time.

While it may appear to be something small but it's, in reality, a massive leap for an improved and more secure internet. Blockstack uses an electronic ledger that tracks usernames and various levels of encryption. The outcome is a higher amount of privacy protection for each user. The blockchain can keep track of domain names, rendering ICANN, the domain oversight body, obsolete. Microsoft is currently engaged with Blockstack to utilize its technology.

While how it handles web-related functions could seem excessive, the lower-level aspects of the internet, in general, have resulted in the dominance of large corporations that have complete freedom to use user data however they wish. The new platform will allow companies to earn profits while also providing services, but the balance of power will be much more favourable for the user than it currently does.

Property rights that are improved, both intangible and tangible property, from homes and cars on the one hand to patents and company shares, on the other, can be connected using blockchain technology and smart contracts to make the process of determining the rights of these items simpler than it currently is. This information can be saved in a kind of ledger that is decentralized, along with the legal details about the actual owner of the asset. The technology may even be extended to intelligent keys, providing specific users access to particular properties.

The ledger will keep track of more specific details and activate certain keys as required. In this scenario, the decentralized ledger is an instrument for storing and managing rights to property and creating duplicates when smart keys disappear.

Utilizing intelligent property protocol can aid in reducing the chance for homeowners to be at risk of fraud, untrustworthy transactions, and the cost of mediation.

New kinds of cash lenders are emerging. With the advent of blockchain technology making it more convenient to transfer money between people and institutions, new lenders for hard cash appear to take advantage of this fact. These lenders offer terms to people with bad credit, but the rates are usually relatively high, and properties are typically classified as collateral. This leads many people to fail on loans, leaving the borrower in a more difficult position than initially. Blockchain-based lending could transform the entire process because the binding nature of the loan means less collateral is needed, and smart contracts will be able to handle the transactions so that costs are reduced.

Smartphones with more intelligent technology: Smartphones run on a kind of cryptography they need the use of your fingerprint image of the face or a password to be activated. It is already a type of intellectual property that is in its infancy. This particular aspect of personal technology is enhanced by blockchain technology because, instead of having these data connected with your actual SIM card, the information will be kept on the blockchain, where they are accessible wherever you happen to be. While security issues could arise in these kinds of scenarios, the fact that every transaction has to be checked before adding it to the chain will ensure that the security of your data is maintained.

Passports Blockchains have helped people to manage passports since at least 2014. They make it simpler for users to recognize themselves, regardless of whether they're offline or online. The system operates by photographing the person using it and then encoding the image using private keys and an open one. The passport is then saved in a public ledger accessible via blockchain addresses by the person with the key.

Important documents No matter if it's a wedding, birth, or death certificate, These documents grant different rights or rights. This wouldn't be so much of a problem if it were not for the fact that the systems that manage the details of these documents are susceptible to errors. According to UNICEF, more than 30% of children below five years of age don't possess birth certificates. Implementing a public blockchain to simplify this process will make tracking these services easier and enable acquiring these documents.

Identification: You currently have to carry your driver's license, your ID card for work, and your Social Security card; the requirements go on and on. If you have a suitable blockchain, all this may be an issue of the past. Sooner or later, everyone will have a unique digital ID that they carry everywhere. It will be linked to a secure global ledger with the most basic information you'll have to move around.

Enhance digital interactions Improve digital interactions: With a greater and greater variety of interactions being conducted online, it's often hard to decide who you can trust.

Blockchain could solve that issue by storing a copy of your identity on an open blockchain to everyone. It will automatically collect things like review scores, rankings, and scores from a vast range of websites so that you'll always have some notion of what you're going to be doing before you take your online interactions into the real world. In contrast to more traditional forms that use social media platforms, people will not be able to delete their data and begin again, as once they are on the blockchain, it will be in the blockchain for all time.

Alter how you fuel your vehicle. Modern electric cars have already made massive progress in fueling. Another significant step is short and is to do with blockchain. Blockchain technology can soon identify the energy a particular owner consumes and automatically remove the cash from the respective account. All the user has to do is go towards the charger, and the blockchain will handle the remainder.

Beyond Cryptocurrency

Fund HIV research Research on HIV Fund: The UBS bank has recently donated Finclusion platform systems. The Inclusion systems will launch the first smart contract, HealBond, which will look for effective trades on the bond market so that the money it generates can support HIV research. Analysts are convinced that with the proper degree of a passive approach, it will be able to start earning profits immediately. If it is successful, it could provide those who have the means to invest in it with many more opportunities to contribute to their preferred causes.

Data security: The firm Factom is focusing on appropriately protecting information. Presently, it's working with the nation of Honduras to make it easier to identify land, and also with many cities in China in what is known as Smart Cities. Blockchain technology is expected to have become an essential tool for getting every system working together at the same time. This could include data notarization and management of information with a greater degree of trust than is accessible to the general public. Factom has already received funds through the US Department of Homeland Security, particularly the Technology and Science Directorate, to research The Blockchain Software to Prove Integrity of Captured Data project.

The power grid should be decentralized: Instead of having a central power provider who has the responsibility of delivering energy to homes and offices, A decentralized blockchain could be created to allow individuals to generate electricity through solar or other methods and then market what they don't require on the open market. Each transaction would be recorded in the Blockchain, limiting fraud to an absolute minimum. With more and more people buying high-capacity batteries for rooftop solar panels, this kind of scenario is rapidly becoming a possibility.

It is challenging to trace. The fact that a blockchain can appear anytime and cannot be changed makes it uniquely competent for monitoring the various kinds of things that are always believed to vanish. For instance, the firm Everledger is currently working on a method to locate particular objects and determine whether or not they're genuine. They have developed a distributed ledger system that examines various diamond transaction verifications, such as law enforcement agencies, insurers, claimants, and owners, to create an overview of the mine of every diamond. This system is advantageous because it helps keep the supply chain accountable and helps consumers assess whether a diamond suits them. Smart contracts also enable diamond transactions to be completed while tracking them, ensuring buyers aren't buying blood diamonds.

Earning artists what they are due instead of worrying about ensuring that their music isn't being used without the right amount of compensation, blockchain musicians are soon able to know who used the song and why, with every single transaction being performed using smart contracts that are facilitated by the blockchain platform. Furthermore, the funds will be distributed immediately instead of waiting for the money to be at a certain level or for someone somewhere to issue checks. The same method can be applied to the licensing of music all-in-all, meaning it is possible to remove intermediaries entirely from the equation. This will result in lower costs for the consumer and increased profits for the artists since people are more likely to purchase content onceagain.

Better communication: If your car is involved in a safety recall, the vehicle manufacturer will send an email to all of its authorized sales outlets. Each one sends out a message tocustomers who purchased the car. This information could be delivered to you and allow you to make an informed choice using the information that you have at your disposal. The recall could be due to something significant or minor, but whatever it is, you'll need to be aware of the issue. Incorporating all the information on blockchains would greatly ease the procedure since after the problem was discovered, the chain would instantly notify the owners in the area of concern.

Understanding the lifecycle of assets Whatever you or the things you're doing, specific tools make life more efficient. Blockchain technology ensures you know everything you can when paired with the Internet of Things. The lifecycle of assets is crucial for anyone from small business entrepreneurs to multi-national corporations. The data offered by this kind of blockchain technology could save lives. Think about, for example, an aircraft that could have different owners throughout its time up in the sky. Blockchains like this will allow the owner to know each part of their aircraft more thoroughly and ensure that the correctmaintenance is carried out throughout its lifespan.

The food chain is being tracked: The increasing accessibility of blockchain technology will mean the slow but steady concerns regarding the quality of food you consume every day will be put to bed. No matter what the final state of the food item when you buy it, you will be able to see the entire path it took to reach your plate. This includes the final product and everything involved in creating the finished product. This is particularly important because there is more to the conventional foodstuff chain than you initially realize. For instance, a farmer may produce that is shipped to a facility for processing, getting to a distribution centre, where it is bought and processed by a different processing facility, only to be bottled in a can filled with tomato soup.

It can alter the worth of your ownership of The Slock. It's business, Slock. It is built upon the Ethereum platform and operates an Ethereum-based blockchain that is called"the Universal Share Network; this network is an open source marketplace that anyone can use to post their assets that arenot being used regardless of whether it's equipment, shipping, containers offices, or other office space. It's an automated AirBnB that can be used for all kinds of things, not just temporary accommodation. Blockchain technology's fundamentals are then transferred to real, tangible assets.

Transportation: A variant in the trend toward crowdsourcing of ridesharing services, La'Zooz is a decentralized transportation platform owned by its customers who use blockchain technology to manage and enhance various intelligent transportation solutions.

Legislative and government officials

All over the world, the government is exploring the various

possibilities that are offered by distributed ledger and blockchain technology. The capability to record and share ledger data quickly and safely has led to the creation of a market for various new methods of government in building trust, stopping fraud, and increasing transparency.

In a recent study conducted by the Economic Intelligence Unit and IBM, it is evident that various governments' enthusiasm for blockchain technology is considerable. As many as 9 of 10 agencies in government are looking to invest in blockchain-based contract management, assets management, regulation compliance, and transaction management before the year. In addition, 7 out of 10 say thatblockchain will likely transform how contracts are managed.

Additionally, more than 20% of respondents believe they will have a blockchain strategy by the end of 2017.

Voting: In in the year election of the 2016 United States general election, both Republicans and Democrats could be heard arguing about how secure the present voting system is. The 2000 presidential election demonstrated that the method by which voting is conducted is outdated. Although concerns over hacking have slowed the adoption of digital voting methods until now, blockchain technology can end those worries. A decentralized public ledger would naturally be protected; however, specific individuals would still be able to verify their vote was counted correctly. This method would not just make it more effective but is also more cost- effective and more secure.

Open, responsive data: The blockchain ledger will also provide an infrastructure for what's commonly referred to as open and responsive data. Research suggests that this kind of data that is freely available could earn more than $3 trillion in one year. Startups will be able to make use of this data to keep ahead of fraudsters.

Parents would be able to get information on the medications they are giving their children, and the list is endless. At present, this kind of information is available through limited, government-approved windows that are not explicitly designed to prioritize the interests of citizens. Since Blockchain is a kind of ledger that is public, people can have access to its information anytime and anywhere.

Auto-management Blockchain offers the possibility for government agencies to manage themselves more efficiently since the exchange of information at a global level will be significantly improved overall. There will be a good amount of trust because the data stored on the blockchain will be available and accessible to everyone.

Lowering administrative costs When property information was uploaded on a blockchain, prospective buyers could more easily quickly and inexpensively confirm ownership details. This is manual, meaning that the government spends thousands of dollars each year to pay individuals doing this work. The manual verification process could also result in more mistakes, costing even more.

It also would significantly reduce how much manual work is required on the bank's part since they'd be required to perform very little work concerning the title insurance. Lenders need title insurance to safeguard their interests. This will lower the cost for homeowners refinancing their home or purchasing their first home, as they will be able to pay less for the entire process since the labour cost will be drastically reduced.

To reduce money laundering, if identity data were easily stored on a cryptocurrency, authorities could more quickly track those who move large sums of money from one location to another. Financial institutions could review every new client's data, which can be passed on to the appropriate authorities if needed. Additionally, storing the information about accounts and payments in the blockchain could be a huge step to make it easier to collect the details required to standardize the type of information necessary to normalize the information needed for an account. This can increase the accuracy of the data being gathered and reduce the number of legitimate transactions mistakenly identified as fraudulent. In addition, having a document deemed secure from tampering would make it much easier for these companies to comply with AML laws.

Ensuring that taxpayers are paid, the Federal Government is likely already developing its type of cryptocurrency. Therefore there's no reason to think they haven't already been developing a method of connecting a blockchain with the existing IRS system. The blockchain will not just keep track of the amount every citizen earned over the past year but also any incentives, grants, subsidies, and loans an individual may be provided in addition to their sources. At the same time, this may result in more people paying higher taxes than they do now, but it will also hold governments accountable for each dollar they earn. It will be easier for money to escape the pockets of bureaucratic purses since a blockchain that anyone can view keeps track of all transactions.

The process of keeping track of incorporation information: Delaware is the first state in the country to allow businesses with incorporated entities to track the rights of shareholders and their capital via blockchain. It is commonplace for companies to be included in Delaware to avail of tax advantages. This can result in a change that will result in various outcomes. Additionally, the state has been transferring its archived records to an open ledger so that more people can access the information for free, at a lower cost for taxpayers.

Digital evidence of residency: In Estonia, well-known for its innovative practices, it's now possible to electronically apply to be a resident of the country with the help of the governmental blockchain. New residents are then issued the digital key card, a cryptographic key used for signing documents with a secure seal that replaces the signatures required on official documents.

Virtual residents can establish bank accounts through Estonia's banking system online, which also uses blockchain technology and allows them to incorporate companies or connect to other electronic services. Estonia is proud of innovating with digital transactions and introducing numerous new financial streams that are being created.

Welfare in the United Kingdom, blockchain has already been converted into a product that is available for purchase through the

Digital Marketplace run by the government. This platform allows various government agencies to explore, test, and develop digital solutions based on blockchain technology and distributed ledgers. In the past, they conducted an experiment with the Department for Work and Pension, which allowed users to benefit from an app for mobile devices that lets users check their monthly benefits payments and transfer their information to a different ledger distributed as a way to assist them in controlling their financials, with approval of course.

Global Blockchain Council: The Global Blockchain Council has been created in Dubai and includes more than 50 private and public organizations that have already started demonstration-of-concept blockchain initiatives in tourism, shipping digital wills, business registration, and title transfer records, and diamond trading. IBM has also joined forces with the council to use IBM's blockchain as the logistics and trade solutions. The Dubai government Dubai has also revealed plans to move all government documents to an integrated blockchain before the year 2020. The anticipated cost savings of this initiative are expected to be 25.1 million person-hours annually.

The Future of BLOCKCHAIN

Blockchain technology is at a stage where anything could occur; it is also a host of issues being developed at a government level that are worth considering when considering the future use of blockchain technology.

Greater control: One of the most significant advantages of blockchain is the ability to work entirely autonomously. But, its ability to function in a way that permitted nearly anonymous transactions made it simple for people interested in skirting legal restrictions. As cryptocurrency gains more recognition as it becomes more popular, governmental and regulatory organizations like the Securities and Exchange Commission, Department of Homeland Security, FBI, and the Financial Crimes Enforcement Network, all in the US, are becoming more aware of its potential to be used in illegal operations.

The amount of scrutiny grew in 2013 after The Financial Crimes Enforcement Network decided that cryptocurrency exchanges were an aspect of a money service business. This meant that they could be subject to government rules. DHS swiftly took advantage of this situation to freeze Mt. Gox's accounts. Mt. Gox, the most significant bitcoin exchange worldwide, is based on allegations of laundering money.

Then, it was followed by a recent SEC decision to block bitcoin from having the possibility of opening an official exchange fund. This increased the value of bitcoin; however, the decrease was followed by a further rise. The decision to deny the application was still under examination as of September 2017. The result is that cryptocurrencies are somewhat of an awkward circumstance as their growing scrutiny makes it more challenging to keep up with their mission despite them being more well-known than ever.

Suppose cryptocurrency ever hopes to become a mainstream degree and eventually be integrated into the existing financial systems. In that case, it must be able to stay in line with its initial goal and yet be complicated enough to withstand the security risks it's sure to face shortly. Furthermore, it needs to be simple enough so that anyone can use it without a problem. In addition, it will need to be decentralized enough to remain identifiable and include different checks and balances to ensure that it is not misused regarding issues like tax fraud. When taken together, the next cryptocurrency will likely have to be a combination of the present form and a traditional currency.

United States: The United States government strives to crack down on those who use blockchain to transfer money. They're not going to be satisfied with this level of control, according to evidence that suggests that they're currently developing their blockchain-based cryptocurrency called Fedcoin. The concept is that Federal Reserve could generate a unique cryptocurrency very quickly. One difference between the crypto they create and others is that it will allow the Federal Reserve to retain the ability to intervene and take out transactions they don't like.

The introduction of the Fedcoin would take place after the block's genesis was created, and the price for Fedcoins was set at 1:1 against the dollars. In time, locating regular dollars will get more challenging until they are eliminated. This could subsequently result in a cryptocurrency independent of its transactions but central in restricting supply and monitoring the various types of transactions.

The Federal Reserve is already on its way to making this dream a reality. They held a closed-door conference with bitcoin regulators in the autumn of 2016. The President of the Federal Reserve sat in on the discussion in person, as did members from Bank for International Settlements, World Bank, and the International Monetary Fund. At this conference, one of the talks was titled "Why Central Banks Will Issue Digital Currencies.

Russia: Russia issued a drastic change to its crypto-police in 2017. Before this, any person who used cryptocurrency was likely to be jailed, and currently, however, the country is fully embracing cryptocurrency. The reason is Russia's high corruption in the banking industry in recent years. Over a hundred banks have been shut down in the last three years, and many money laundering scams cannot be stopped.

To be able to monitor better where their money moving To better monitor where its money is going, Russian authorities are currently developing various blockchain- based technology applications to make it simpler to keep track of real-time transactions. It appears they're less interested in creating a new digital currency and are more focused on the distributed ledger component of blockchain technology. There is no information yet on whether Russia intends to build an entirely new blockchain or use an existing blockchain to serve its purposes.

China: China is currently an essential supporter of the field of blockchain. In June 2017, China's People's Bank of China released an official news report on the development of its digital currency, which has the potential to expand dramatically based on the volume of transactions each day. Although all the details aren't yet disclosed, several sources suggest that the bank will likely make the currency available worldwide in conjunction with its renminbi initiative. Although no official release date is expected, the money is moving forward in its development process and is already seeing testing with many commercial banks in the country and The People's Bank. This is an enormous advancement for recognized blockchains and cryptocurrencies of all sorts. It also shows how determined China has been to the concept of thoroughly investigating the world of digital currencies.

The cryptocurrency they make is expected to bring significant economic benefits to the country. This is because it's backed by the People's Bank, which means it is functionally similar to the banknote but with fewer associated charges. It also could be well to get bankingservices in China to

Today, many of its residents cannot access traditional financial services.

CRYPTOCURRENCY AS WELL AS BLOCKCHAININTERACTIONS

Blockchain technology could perform a variety of things soon; the primary thing you'll be able to remember is that blockchains have made cryptocurrency feasible, and bitcoin increased in value by up to $2,000 this summer. Although this price has put bitcoin out of the realm of many investors who are not experts, There are over 1,000 different available cryptocurrency options; therefore, there are many possibilities for those looking to make money from an investment. However, this doesn't mean that there's no risk too it's crucial to keep the dangers of investing in cryptocurrency in mind and be aware of the risks before investing in this area.

Pros

Lowers the chance of identity theft: Since the cryptocurrency is digital and therefore, is subject to a lower risk of identity theft than conventional forms of currency. They cannot be counterfeited or counterfeited, and transactions can't be altered to ensure that the transaction never occurred due to the blockchain. Furthermore, once you've invested in a cryptocurrency, you can move it around quickly without worrying about dealings with fake people or companies who put your information in areas they wouldn't like. For most exchanges, there is no authentication whatsoever when you already have cryptocurrency. For most businesses, even without cryptocurrency, creating a debit or credit transaction is necessary each time you make financing.

Accessibility It is estimated that there are 3.5 billion people with access to the internet and don't have any reliable method of banking. This is a market blockchain technology is trying to tap into to the maximum extent possible and will bring about significant growth in the sector in the future as cryptocurrency becomes prevalent. If this kind of banking becomes popular, those who invest in cryptocurrency in the early days are likely to earn much more than a few dollars and could make profits on a large scale.

Cost-effective: Although every cryptocurrency transaction comes with a cost, the costs for this kind of exchange are usually less than when you make an exchange through the traditional broker site.

Cons

Technology advancements: While bitcoin has been a good investment over the last few years, the cryptocurrency market is very untested in general, meaning that its risks remain unclear compared to the more traditional markets. Naturally, this makes the highs that the markets experience more potent than comparable markets, but it also makes the lows more dramatic. There's no guarantee that one will become another, and trends may be triggered in unexpected patterns that nobody has ever witnessed. The thing it comes with is that it lacks the correct information for us to accurately forecast where the market is going to be within a year or even five. As long as the market doesn't stabilize, it is impossible to know if each dollar you invest will be worth

$2 in a year or if it will turn out to cost $.02.

Extreme volatility Bitcoin, considered the most robust cryptocurrency, is five times higher in volatility than gold. It is seven times more volatility than if put that money in the S&P 500. In contrast, this means that you stand a better likelihood of earning profits, but it also means that the possibility of losing will be significantly more than it should be. It is essential to realize that most transactions are for speculation purposes. That means the cryptocurrency is bought by investors, not those who plan to utilize it daily. This implies that prices will likely be higher than the actual demand and supply market suggests. The phenomenon of early adopters means that people who purchase early will experience a price increase; however, the upward trend isn't last. This isn't about whether but the question of the time.

Physicality is not a factor: Although cryptos are indeed a digital payment method, one of its most prominent characteristics, the reality is that the concept itself poses difficulties. Particularly, think about the possibility that the server is not physically located; it could be a problem.

When the security of your cryptocurrency is compromised, If your cryptocurrency is lost and there is no backup plan, your investment is lost forever. You have a range of ways to place in charge of the cryptocurrency into your control; however, the reality is that a physical currency will always be more accessible to hold than one that is digital.

The enormous potential for earning money in hacking into blockchains means that hackers aren't ceased trying to achieve this. The other thing this means is that they're occasionally likely to succeed. For instance, it is the case that the Ethereum platform has indeed been the victim of various attacks over its existence. One of them was so successful that it required the creation of a hard fork, which resulted in the Ethereum blockchain split between the ones that made money from the attack and those that were disadvantaged by it. The dollar's value is not going to be split. It is not likely to happen regardless of how many dollars are taken in the case of a bank robbery, which shows how risky deciding to invest in a new business opportunity is.

Trading in cryptocurrency

Whatever familiarity you are with traditionally-based securities, trading on the cryptocurrency market could prove very profitable so long as you accept the risk of trading. Be aware that it is essential never to invest funds that you aren't able to risk losing. There are not many barriers to entry, and as we mentioned earlier, if you already own cryptocurrency, you don't have to consider confirming your account.

Another advantage of trading on this market is that there aren't any centralized exchanges, meaning each trade competes independently. This makes the market highly dispersed, naturally making spreads more extensive than you'll find elsewhere. The lack of regulation implies that it is pretty easy to locate a wide margin, which means small investments can yield significant amounts of money more quickly than different types of investments. Still, the same can be said for losses too. In addition, depending on the currency you're trading with, you'll likely get it at different rates on various exchanges, which implies that you could make money by buying them in one location and then selling them elsewhere.

The most commonly used method to trade cryptocurrency through an exchange company is through contracts for differences. This kind of contract binds buyers and sellers for the duration of the contract. Once it expires and the buyer pays sellers, the gap between the product's value will be at the close of the agreement and the value at the time of the contract's beginning. If the price fluctuates in the opposite direction, the seller must give the buyer the amount. In the case of securing leverage, you'll probably get rates of more than 20 times one, but it is not advised that you search for them until you're entirely familiar with how to trade in this market.

Global currency In the case of conventional money, the amount of factors that could affect the price naturally is going to be pretty small. In contrast, many factors can affect the price.

For cryptocurrencies, however, it's challenging to know what's likely to alarm investors before it happens. Every currency news could result in prices that are drastically changing. In reality, many of the most notable moves in bitcoin resulted from the introduction of capital controls in Greece and when China reduced the value of the Yuan.

The market is always open: Although Forex is typically considered to be the most secure market because it is available for trading all day every week, however, the cryptocurrency market is public all 168 hours of the week, and trading is always taking place regardless of the region in which the world is operating. Currently, there are around 100 cryptocurrency exchanges worldwide, all of which offer different trading levels and rates depending on the level of service they provide. So, it should not require more than a few minutes of study to determine the best one for you.

This could also be interpreted as a negative based on risk tolerance since these elements could cause massive daily swings. In reality, price swings more remarkable than 5 per cent are typical on the majority of days for more significant cryptocurrencies. The smaller ones should not be too shocked if they have an increase of 15 per cent or more.

Find your exchange

When deciding to commit to a particular exchange, it is crucial to conduct the necessary research you require to feelconfident about your choice. If you don't do enough research could lead to you being in a position where your exchange suddenly disappears without your money, or you discover that the business does not have enough money to meet its obligations. Then there's an uproar since everyone is desperate to recover their money in one go. If something like this occurs, remember that you'll have no recourse, especially if you pick an exchange that isn't situated in your own country. This is why the first decision you make could be so important.

Make sure that transparent exchanges are prioritized. Generally, the finer the trade you select is willing to become, the higher in line with the quality it's likely to be. This means that you're likely to want to examine the order book of their company, which is essentially a copy that is a distributed ledger. It displays how much is sold or bought frequently. It's also possible to inquire about where the money is held and the method they use to verify the appropriate amount of reserve currency. If you're having a hard in obtaining answers to these simple questions, then the exchange may simply not be able to disclose that information. Conversely, it could indicate that they're a fractional exchange and cannot pay their liabilities. When selecting the most appropriate cryptocurrency exchange, it's better to be secure than not.

Secure and available: It is essential to choose an exchange that has a high-security level because, after all, as we've mentioned, your cryptocurrency earnings won't be able to be available outside of this exchange without your help, so security is of paramount significance. You should only select discussions that include HTTPS at the beginning of their URL, as it indicates they're using an encrypted protocol, which implies that they are working hard to protect your account information.

To prevent theft. It is also essential to ensure that your exchange uses a two-factor authentication method and standard safe login methods. If your account isn't this secure, you could risk stealing your identity and money.

Fees add up: Nearly every cryptocurrency comes with prices that are paid. Part of it is delivered to the owner of the blockchain platform, while the rest is paid to the miner or miners who verify your transactions. Although these fees are voluntary, they usually remove some of the motivation for the transaction to be confirmed, which could mean that the whole process will take longer than it would normally. The business will be required if you don't choose an exchange in China. With all the fees floating around, they could be pretty costly, so you must be prepared with a plan for trading to follow before making your first trade to avoid losing a substantial part of your capital due to charges.

Choose a local option: While there are numerous cryptocurrency exchanges across the globe, you should try to find one in your own country, If you can. This is beneficial in many ways, one benefit being you'll most likely be in a position to make use of the times when there are more volumes simply because you'll be in the same time zone as the exchange. A local conversation can help if you ever need to reach support, and deposits are processed more quickly also. Additionally, based on the location of your country and laws, there could be some kind of oversight of cryptocurrency exchanges, which means that getting your money back following a suspicious business may not be entirely out of the question.

When selecting an exchange in your area, check that they provide the cryptocurrency pairs you're looking for. Sales can vary significantly from one business to the next, and there's no guarantee that you'll be able to exchange your country's currency regardless of a company near your home.

Be aware of transaction times: Since every cryptocurrency transaction must verify and added to the cryptocurrency before it can be cleared, exchanges usually perform with a short period to let the process breathe. Selecting a business with acceptable transaction speed is essential to get the most effective outcomes. Additionally, you're likely to be looking to ensure your purchase remains fixed no matter the time it takes to complete. If this isn't the case, you're at risk of doing a deal that appears promising only to see price fluctuations and cause problems before the transaction happens.

Well-known exchanges

Kraken: It is a European exchange that manages the most quantity of euro transactions each day. They are also among the top 15 in terms of USD exchanges, too.

Coinbase Coinbase is the most senior cryptocurrency exchange in the US and is regarded as the most extended continuously operating USD exchange. It is well-known for its strict adherence to regulations and remains among the top five in the volume of transactions per day.

OKCoin The OKCoin is a USD exchange located in Japan; this means that they are subject to lower regulations than the other exchanges listed on this list. If you're looking to get more margins and fewer charges and are happy with the additional risk, this is the perfect exchange.

Bitstamp has been operating continuously since 2011, and it is the second most utilized USD exchange, with a daily volume of more than 10,000 units per day.

Bitfinex is the exchange that handles the most significant amount of USD trading in terms of quantity of all businesses in the world, and it clears more than 200,000 bitcoins worth of cryptocurrency each week. If you're thinking of taking this route but aren't sure the moment you own cryptocurrency, then it is possible to begin without submitting any verification form.

Initial coin offerings (ICOs)

In 2017 a blockchain-based firm raised over $150 million in just 24 hours. In another company, Status. I'd managed half that amount. The outpourings of generosity from investors are referred to as Initial coin offerings. Like all things associated with cryptocurrency, they present an enormous risk with a potentially lucrative reward. In the summer of 2017, the process generated over $500 million.

While it's a variation on the phrase "initial public offering, "the initial coin offering differs in every aspect. A coin offering in its initial stages is a form of crowdfunding that allows blockchain companies to sell their cryptocurrency at a highly investor-friendly cost. Then investors purchase it in the hopes of seeing its price increase to as low as 50 cents. At the very least, the company will have the funds to complete its endeavour and then launch it to the market with the hope that its product or service is so well-liked that the cost of its cryptocurrency will increase due to the increased demand. It is worth noting that the Ethereum platform has already established itself as the most favoured platform for businesses planning to launch their first cryptocurrency offering.

The bulk of this cash is currently coming from China Investors from all over the globe have been recognized to cash out their checks in the event of a reasonable price. Although investing in what is essentially an unknown amount always is not without risk, Initial coin offerings can be riskier nonetheless. This is because they do not fall covered by the SEC regulatory framework, meaning that the business plans they are preparing aren't subject to the same scrutiny as those who submit applications to an initial public offer. There is also the possibility that the success the first coin offerings enjoyed may be due to a different bubble, which makes it likely to fail.

Although they have problems, they can also yield substantial profits for investors who make the right choices at the right time. However, if you're considering investing in this kind of venture, you must be aware that if you decide on investment in an initial coin sale, you're making one of the riskiest investment choices.

To mitigate the risk in the least amount feasible, you'll have to approach any initial coin offerings with a sceptical attitude. The first thing to do is review all the information the company has made public, which could include an operating plan. It will be simpler to judge the feasibility of a project from a financial perspective and make sure that the business plan is viable in the long run. Also, you must be aware that the marketplace will want the service or product the company is planning to offer. Additionally, you'll want to be sure and know the purpose of the cryptocurrency you're buying into once the service or product is in operation.

It is also important to remember that buying in the initial offering of coins is likely to differ from purchasing the initial public offerings. If you buy into the former, you are left with ownership shares that represent that you have a tiny part of the business you are buying into. Initial coin offerings give you none of these rights but the possibility of acquiring digital currency that could or might not be worth anything. Furthermore, the first public offerings are subject to stricter conditions imposed on them, including requirements for accreditation and fiduciary duties, which the company has to meet before it can launch its offerings; however, none of this is needed for initial coin offerings.

You're likely to never see beyond a paper, a business plan, or a website from an initial coin offering business or all of them. Likely, they are not expected to have a prototype or product to showcase, so you're likely to have to take a lot of the information they provide you on the wing. Also, you must remember that just because a first coin offering receives a positive number of responses early doesn't mean that this positive impression will last beyond the day it goes live and even longer. It is also important to note that many experts believe that the risk of giving companies too much money too early

Limits their possibilities as owners feel pressure to spend every dollar they can while feeling less motivated to create an actual product.

The list of shady IoCs spans from those with unrealistic expectations to complete scams with the sole aim of taking your hard-earned money. There is a growing number of ICOs with just an attractive website with buzzwords and high valuations based solely on their personal opinion. The most important thing you must consider before investing is the actual potential of the idea. What solutions to a specific issue does the company claim to address? And more importantly, what is the problem in the first place that calls for blockchain technology? It is essential to look at the group that is behind the project, as well as, in particular, their previous experience with similar projects to that. Another critical factor to consider is whether the token they're offering has a benefit for the project. Are investors planning to sell it to make profits once it's on the market? Also, you should look out for big bonuses for early investors. It's not unusual for a pre-sale reward to be provided; however, should these bonuses surpass 100 per cent, you could be a bit suspicious about what the motivation is for those who aren't early adopters and whether the company is just looking to make as much money as fast as they can. One advantage that the Ethereum platform has is the possibility of allowing intelligent contracts that can be integrated into the ICO, for example, the money held in a system similar to escrow to ensure that they are returned investors if the founders of the project fail to adhere to the terms of the contract.

Then one should note that the vast majority of current profitable initial coin offerings are founded upon the Ethereum blockchain platform, which means that the foundation of these companies is an untested technology. Although Ethereum blockchain technology has a better chance of making it than the Ethereum blockchain platform is more likely to achieve it than the majority of other platforms companies, the reality of the issue is that it's not yet tested. Hence, there's still the possibility of a downside and upside.

In the end, it could be a good idea to wait and see how the initial round of the initial coin offering firms go before getting directly involved in the type of investment.

Tips for investing successfully

Although investing in cryptocurrency may be as simple as finding an exchange and then putting an amount of money in the machine, actually making a profit from your investment is quite a different story. The next step is to create an outline of the things you should be aware of to make investments that are successful in the long run.

It's an asset: The initial thing you'll be required to do is think about cryptocurrency the same way as you think of every other kind of commodity. Like any other commodity, cryptocurrency is utilized for both practical and investments, the same way precious metals can be used in commercial applications and base metals can be used for industrial purposes. Furthermore, they mostly traded on exchanges that adhere to the same guidelines. To select the most likely to grow in value, you will need to choose the most likely to give you the most excellent real-world value or have the highest potential uses beyond P2P transactions.

Increased usage: When taken in a unified manner, all of the current cryptocurrencies have a market value of around $160 billion. They're in the same category as big companies like Tesla and Microsoft in terms of numbers. This number is fascinating because real-world use and a growing market cap have been in sync. Studies indicate that cryptocurrency and blockchain usage will only rise in the next five years.

This is when market saturation is likely to happen and will likely be at the point when many of the present bubbles fail at first. While the market remains very volatile in the short term, the long-term potential of cryptocurrency as an investment should be reasonably stable. The possibility of growth is evident from the market cap's perspective.

Staggering. The price of cryptocurrency worldwide is bound to continue going upwards. And, when the number of users is stable, investors won't need to be concerned about the effects of the bubble since prices are likely to stop rapidly at this moment too.

The point in the Market cycle is a kind of investment pattern each investment will go through at some point. On the bright side, it begins with optimism, before moving on to the excitement, before reaching a peak of euphoria. Then it decreases due to fear, anxiety, denial, depression, and panics. Once it has reached its bottom, it rises again by overcoming depression, hope, and relief before finding optimism.

While bitcoin has gone through the cycles multiple times, the last one being this year's crash majority of cryptocurrencies are in the optimistic stage, so there's ample time for you to start investing as the opportunities are plentiful. If you conduct your research right at the beginning, there's no reason to believe that you can't get five years of reliable increase in your investment before hitting the peak of excitement.

While this is good news, it's essential to remember that today's cryptocurrency market is similar to the dot-com boom in the 1990s. This means that around 80 per cent of the cryptos available are likely to fail before or after the market reaches its saturation level. This is because there are only an array of options in a small market. Only a few are likely to last the escalating price. A lot of investors will be tempted to throw their money at a business but not know what the company's actual activities are as the economy will fall because of this; however, when you are aware of what's to come, you'll be able to stay clear of the worst.

The key to solving problems is to solve them. No matter the possibility of gaining from a specific cryptocurrency, investing in it and then lying and waiting for it to take its course isn't the most profitable strategy for making money. Instead, you'll be better off investing effort into finding the right cryptocurrency.

Cryptocurrency can solve issues that affect individual markets or, more importantly, the entire world. The more complex the problem is resolved, the more likely it will become worthwhile to invest in in the long run. It is crucial to look at solutions to banking services that many parts of the world consider standard. Cryptocurrencies that offer solutions for paying for transactions and wire money will be excellent choices in the coming years.

Long-term perspective: Given the magnitude of changes you are likely to experience regularly, The ideal cryptocurrency portfolio will be focused exclusively on the long-term. It is also expected that you'll have to take the initiative to select a range of different cryptocurrencies that you can invest your money in. between three or five, so that you don't get significantly impacted by massive fluctuations in one location or the other. Above all else, it will be essential to manage your emotions as well as you can and work to avoid making unwise choices when investing is at stake. When you first get into the game, it's an excellent decision not to keep an eye on the investments you make too much because they're likely to be scattered all around the place. Keep in mind that the long-term investment objective is to maintain a steady upward trend, which means that some fluctuation is expected.

It is also crucial to keep in mind that cryptocurrency does not carry the risk of locking in what other investments that are long-term do. Suppose you believe that the right time to invest in a specific cryptocurrency is here. In that case, you can quickly and conveniently trade it in any currency of your choice instead of changing it in an older fashion in the down market. Therefore, you might be interested in investing in cryptocurrencies like saving money into a savings account and one that offers an increased chance of the return you can expect from your investment.

TOP 10 CRYPTO CHOICES TO BUY

If you're looking to make an investment opportunity in the market for cryptocurrency, There are the top 10 ones! They offer distinct advantages when compared with other cryptocurrencies. Certain have more excellent stability than others, and some don't require mining.

1.   Ethereum (ETH) is the second most well-known coin, but it also has its platform

Ethereum is one of the most well-known cryptocurrencies, second only to Bitcoin in trading, and could be a wise investment. It's not just a currency but also a platform that operates with its money that can be used to pay for services offered within the Ethereum system. The system functions by ensuring that every transaction is funded by Ether (the title of the currency) to operate; in essence, Ethereum is an operating system that runs another cryptocurrency. This means it will provide more excellent stability than Bitcoin since it functions as the computer's power source, and you don't need to purchase expensive mining equipment to minethe coin.

2. NEO (NEO) is the Chinese variant of Ethereum

At present, NEO is still relatively new and was only launchedrelatively recently. It is, therefore, less expensive than Ethereum and offers some positives over Bitcoin. NEO is a highly efficient way to operate decentralized transactions in

the digital world. Its perspective on blockchain assists in solving many of the problems currently facing Bitcoin, like the high cost of commerce, the slow processing times, and expensive transaction costs.

3. Ripple (XRP) is an official currency for cross-border transactions. There's one cryptocurrency I can envision being used to pay for anything other than Bitcoin, Ether Ripple, or XRP. It's the only cryptocurrency with an exchange of its currency and wallet. It's been used for cross-border transactions for a long time, and its creators consider it good money. My opinion is that even if in the future it becomes possible to exchange an alternative cryptocurrencywith XRP, I believe that XRP is widely accepted as a currency that is worth buying.

4. Bitcoin (BTC) The most prestigious cryptocurrency ever

Bitcoin is often referred to as the very first decentralized cryptocurrency. It was invented by an unidentified programmer who goes by the name of Satoshi Nakamoto in the year 2009, which was quite early in the crypto field. In comparison to various currencies, Bitcoin can be highly volatile. It is not a suitable choice for trading based on price stability. However, its early historical position is now the most trusted cryptocurrency, built on blockchain technology.

5. Ethereum Classic (ETC) - The first Ethereum as well as the sole one that has an actual community

Ethereum Classic is a cryptocurrency created by the first Ethereum founder, who resigned from the Ethereum project because of differences with fellow members about improving the system (in particular, scalability). It is a part of the Ethereum Community; however, it has been split into two groups, in the same manner as Bitcoin split and split into Bitcoin as well as Bitcoin Classic. Ethereum Classic is based on the concept of maintaining a blockchain that can be unchangeable and will keep the initial protocol.

6. Stellar Lumens (XLM) - Based on Ripple but with a larger community

Stellar Lumens are often compared with Ripple since they share a lot of similarities in their technology as well as in their communities. Both have large communities behind the platform and more than one billion coins. The primary difference between them can be seen in the fact they both use Stellar Lumens, which is Stellar Lumens is open-source and has more transparency in its development experience. It is important to note that both contain over one million tokens, and it is difficult to anticipate future price changes because of the enormous supply.

7. OmiseGO (OMG) The OMG cryptocurrency has a lot of potential

OmiseGO was developed by the same team that created Ethereum and is supported by an already established company (also known as Omise). The cryptocurrency will be backed by a bank and an entity in Thailand known as Krungsri Bank. It aims to be a decentralized exchange that allows payments between users without fees. It's also the only one that has been tested and is extremely simple to use. In the past, this cryptocurrency was considered the frontrunner of Ethereum on the Ethereum network. It also boasted a large community and an incredibly successful token sale.

8. Litecoin (LTC) is the most well-known cryptocurrency

Litecoin is among the oldest cryptocurrency available, just like Bitcoin. However, unlike Bitcoin, it was primarily geared towards everyday transactions and not just speculation. It does not use blockchain technology but instead employs the same algorithm used by Bitcoin; however, the blocks are generated more quickly. It was introduced in 2011 and was initially believed to be an "altcoin that could improve Bitcoin's technology. Litecoin differentiates itself from Bitcoin in that it is a lot more valuable than other cryptocurrencies while being a part of a larger community.

9. Monero (XMR) is a privacy cryptocurrency with a vast community

Monero is a highly new cryptocurrency introduced in 2014 and built-in blockchain tech. It makes use of ring signaturesto hide transactional information. The cryptocurrency is anonymous that utilizes unique cryptography to hide details of transactions such as the sender, recipient, as well as the transaction's branch. It does not have a foundation in blockchain technology but is a decentralized cryptocurrencythat is a private currency.

10.   Cardano (ADA) This digital currency has a lot of potential

Cardano was developed by the same people who founded Ethereum and is based on their intelligent contracts but emphasizes decentralization. It is a virtual currency called ADA (the symbol for the money). It is used to make payments on the platform, which will be comparable with Ethereum's Ether. Cardano is an up-and-coming cryptocurrency with the potential to eventually take over Ethereum as the most popular system for smart contracts. The community is highly active and has witnessed many partnerships with corporations like IBM.

www.ingramcontent.com/pod-product-compliance
Lightning Source LLC
Chambersburg PA
CBHW060037210326
41520CB00009B/1166